AF430296

Practical Prepping For Everyday People

A common sense guide to preparing for life's emergencies

Mark and Krista Lawley

Copyright 2020

All Rights Reserved

Table Of Contents

Dedication

We dedicate this book to our dear friend, Officer Nick O'Rear, a Kimberly, Alabama police officer whose life was taken in the line of duty, February 5, 2020.

In addition to being a police officer, he had worked as a firefighter and as 1an Emergency Medical Technician. He thrived on helping others in their time of need.

He was a fellow HAM radio operator, (KK4IGB), and would regularly respond to the Emergency Operations Center or an emergency shelter to provide communications during and after severe weather events. Nick was one of the volunteers mentioned in this book that was camping in the woods providing communications and protecting lives at the Yellowhammer Endurance horse ride.

He was always willing to help others, do more than his share, be a team player, and offer encouragement and humor at just the right moment. He was a good man, a good friend, and a good soul. His contributions to this book are significant, and we are forever blessed for having known him.

We love you, we miss you, and we know that we will see you again.

Mark and Krista

Preface

As we are finishing up this book, the world is in the midst of the Coronavirus COVID-19 crisis. We have seen many things and learned many lessons that will apply directly to the practical prepper.

One lesson was the suddenness of "panic-buying" behavior in the stores. Though we cannot figure out exactly why the hot commodity was initially toilet paper, the shelves emptied quickly as people loaded up carts with a year's worth of paper goods. We saw on local social media sites several people who said they were down to one or two rolls of toilet paper before the crisis hit, and were asking for help in finding even a couple of rolls.

Over the next few days not only was toilet paper lacking on the shelves but also the meat counters were emptied and the shelves of bottled water became barren.

As the country went into "lock-down", as some called it, runs on grocery stores ramped up to the point that canned good aisles were looking empty.

Many people were unprepared and panic-bought a month's worth of food and supplies, causing budget problems, incurring debt, and creating hardship for other consumers, like the elderly, or food pantries.

Many people were laid-off when businesses were ordered closed, and some of those were already living pay-check-to-pay-check, and experienced financial hardship trying to get prepared to care for their families.

Preparing ahead of time is the lesson learned here. Our system of prepping had us ready, and can have you ready as well, for the next 'crisis' we WILL face. Think about the peace that will come knowing you don't have to fight the crowds of panic-buyers. Think about the peace of knowing you can feed your family for one, two, three months or more with no paycheck coming in.

Another lesson learned through this is how our current heathcare system operates under the crushing demands of a pandemic. The scale and sudden timeline staggered even the largest hospitals and emptied the national stockpiles of PPE (personal protective equipment). The Centers for Disease Control (CDC) estimate the demands for PPE and testing kits on "normal" seasons of flu, strep, measles, staph, MRSA, RSV, and so on. However, the COVID-19 threat loomed large, quickly dominating all news media, with demands for hundreds of thousands of test kits, hospital bed space, ventilators, increased medical staff, and a national shutdown of "non-essential" businesses, plunging millions into unemployment and uncertainty. Public and private schools were closed, forcing millions of students and parents to homeschool; a new term was coined— "social distancing", staying 6-10 feet away from others in public places to minimize exposure and contact. Corona virus canceled the 2020 Summer Olympics in Tokyo!

Few could imagine the scale of need and the exorbitant costs associated with a global pandemic. This was intensified by the amazingly short time frame from identification of the virus and the rapid need for treatment of thousands of patients to the directives of social distancing and public-gathering limitations coming from local and federal leaders.

All the while, the usual health issues continued. Heart attacks and strokes continued to happen. Broken bones and other injuries continued. Gall bladders and appendixes chose to take the opportunity to flare up. Being spring, the pollen-induced allergies were in full swing, seasonal flu and bronchitis were rampant, and babies were born. Life goes on.

The lesson here is to keep ourselves as healthy as we can, to boost our immune systems, and to keep a supply of over-the-counter medications on hand to treat minor illness on our own. A good first-aid kit lets us handle those relatively minor injuries and burns without having to seek outside medical attention. A good multi-vitamin and some sort of regular exercise is a must, especially for those of us in the less than youthful (not quite over-the-hill but we can see it from here) group.

Before this hit, lots of folks made fun of "preppers." Much of this came from the portrayal of preppers on TV. Producers found the most eccentric folks out there for their shows; those who built bunkers and stored twenty-five years' worth of food, storing Geiger counters, HAZMAT suits, gas masks, and preparing for the-end-of-the-world-as-we-know-it, or TEOTWAKI. Those are not the practical preppers. The practical prepper is the neighbor next door or across the street, those who quietly put back enough food, water and supplies to provide for their family through an extended local emergency.

Today, fewer people are laughing at the practical preppers; in fact, many are wishing they had been *more* prepared. It is our aim to help others become prepared for the next crisis, which WILL come.

Introduction

This book is designed to:

- Help you develop emergency plans

- Guide you as you in your prepping journey

- Cause you to make a logical threat assessment

- Encourage you to take your prepping to the next level

The goal of this book is to provide guidance in equipping yourself with the ability to handle emergencies at home, on the road, or in a strange place. It is not about teaching you skills, but helping you identify the items, equipment, skills, abilities, and means you may need to get through an emergency.

In 2019, America endured over 500 tornadoes in thirteen days from the mid-west to New York, and parts of the mid-west experienced devastating floods. Lives were lost. Towns were destroyed. Life for many Americans changed. News sources reported approximately fifty-eight million people were affected directly or were in this threat's path.

Millions were without power, water, and the basic necessities of life. Help is dispatched immediately, but, due to damaged infrastructure or destroyed cell towers, that type of help may take several days, even a week or more, to arrive.

This book will help you get prepared to stay alive after major disasters until help comes, but will also help prepare you to handle many of life's emergencies which may seem large at the time yet pale in comparison to those impacted by cataclysmic storms. How often have you heard someone wish out loud, "I should have been more prepared"?

Some personal life events are so devastatingly disastrous that they cannot be adequately covered in this book.

- The death of a loved one

- Health problems

- Serious accidental injury

Some natural disasters could be so severe or so large that no amount of prepping will guarantee or even increase the chance of survival, if you are within or close to the impact area.

- Massive wild fire

- Asteroid impact

- Super volcano

Some man-made disasters are so destructive that the only prepping that will bring survival is to not be near where it happens.

- Nuclear explosion or attack

- Large dam break

- Total societal collapse or urban violence

- Some acts of terrorism

Granted, proper practical prepping can and will help you survive after the event, IF you survive the initial threat.

Depending on your age, family situation, world-view, personal or religious beliefs, there may be some events that you might rather not survive.

We feel rather certain that, in an all-out nuclear attack, the city we in which live would be a major target. Since we have already discussed our game plan, should this attack actually happen, we'll share that with you now; we would each pour a large glass of iced tea, select a comfortable patio chair, sit in the yard and watch the fireworks. There is no place locally we could survive, and no distance we could travel in that time frame to keep us safe, and we don't believe that we could enjoy life after such a catastrophic event. Why would we even want to? We believe that there is life after this life, and we believe that we have made preparations for eternity. We would rather just go ahead and enter that life rather than try to survive what would surely be a non-survivable event for us here.

Chapter 1

Who Is A Prepper?

A "prepper" is someone who "prepares", whether it is for a day, week, month, or several years. The word "prepper" is a modern term, but the concept of preparing or storing goods is not new at all; in fact, our grandparents and great-grandparents stored up necessary provisions and resources as did their ancestors for generations. Coal chutes were built into the foundations of big-city apartment houses to fuel huge furnaces during bitterly cold winters; root cellar shelves were crowded with jars of vegetables, grains, and fruits preserved with care from a bountiful garden harvest. They referred to this practice as "plain old common sense".

Life on the farm historically meant the farmer had to have the tools and materials to make repairs on whatever broke. There were no big-box home improvement stores or local hardware shops nearby, so the farmer also had to be a mechanic, blacksmith, and engineer. They had to put up enough food to supply the family when harvest time had ended. When the crops came in, they went about "jar-canning", dehydrating fruits, making beef jerky, salt-curing hams, and so on. They raised in the summer and were sustained through the winter. Our great-grandparents were 'preppers' before the term was established.

Anyone can become a prepper, and it does not require establishing a homestead or living "off the grid". It can be done in an apartment, mobile home, camper or RV. In recent years, we've seen a sharp rise in the number of hobby farmers keeping chickens, ducks, honeybees, fish ponds, rabbits, lambs and goats for food and profit; many also cultivate fruit orchards and vegetable gardens for their families or local markets, making them profitable practical preppers!

Preppers anticipate emergencies, and choose not to depend on luck or society to take care of their needs. We're seeing more disaster events that cause major power outages for longer periods of time, less access to clean water sources, shortages of shelter and food for greater numbers of people occurring at an increasing rate, with a growing population woefully unprepared to survive for even a few days. To think ahead, as in long-term scenarios, days, weeks, even as far as months and years, *is* the mindset of a prepper.

Prepper Stereotypes

"*The Homesteader*" - Raises much of their own vegetables in a garden, keeps chickens for fresh eggs and meat, maybe breeds rabbits, and builds an impressive compost pile. Often says, "I will live off my land for years. I'm not leaving for any reason, regardless of how bad it gets."

"*The Paul Bunyan*" - The loner, "I'll do everything by myself. I'll live in the woods or at a bug-out location for the duration. I have enough wood to last three years and an axe to cut more. I'll hunt, trap, and forage to live off the land. I'm a survivalist."

"*The Tin Hatter*" - they believe everything is a conspiracy. Big Brother is watching. "The government is listening to all our conversations, reading our emails, and monitoring all communications. They have lied to us about aliens, 'chemtrails', the moon landing, and deep state; FEMA is setting up camps to house all the sheeple when the time comes."

"The "*Holy Roller*" - "God told me to get ready for the great apocalypse and to tell you to get ready. If you believe what I believe and do the things I do, you will be protected when it hits the fan. Otherwise, you are toast."

"*The Doomsdayer*" - A cousin to the 'tin hatter,' this prepper prepares for that one singular event which they believe will wipe out 90% of the earth's population, and end life as we know it. The term is TEOTWAWKI- 'the end of the world as we know it'. Some of these folks build underground bunkers to withstand avian flu, nuclear blasts, EMP (man-made electromagnetic pulse wiping out the power grid), societal collapse causing hoards of 'takers' leaving the cities, a pandemic, or a zombie apocalypse. They store enough food, water, power generators, and gas masks to last for years, and have equipment and methods to replenish and protect it.

"The *Daytripper*"- they'll buy bread and milk when the weather folks use the snow word. They pick up a jar of peanut butter and a pack of sandwich meat to go with the bread and milk. When a hurricane is headed their way, they'll buy food, water, and batteries, locate their flashlights and fill the gas tank. They'll likely buy plywood to board up the windows. Then after the storm, they use those supplies up over the year, not keeping any year around.

"*The Panicked Store-Hopper*" – akin to the "Daytripper", they're driven by fear created by media hype about what is disappearing from the shelves. The Panicked Store-Hopper goes from store to store in search of that item they are told they need and if they find it they buy more than they could possibly need. We saw this with toilet tissue in the Covid-19 pandemic. People walked into the store and when told there was no toilet tissue turned around and walked out. If they found it, they would buy two thirty-six roll packages.

"*The Practical Prepper*" - The average Joe or Jane who takes the Boy Scout motto, "Be Prepared" to heart and makes common-sense preparations to be self-sufficient for a reasonable amount of time, and doesn't want to depend on the government in order to feed their families, withstand a job loss, or survive in the weeks after a hurricane, blizzard, or ice storm. They prepare to stay warm and eat when the power goes out. They are also prepared to handle many of the usual "emergencies" which come into our daily lives... flat tires, dead car batteries, extended grid-locked situations.

Practical preppers prepare for natural disasters, job loss, financial or societal upheaval, as well as life's "little everyday emergencies."

They'll equip the car with a first-aid kit, jumper cables or "jump box", small fire extinguisher, rain gear, snacks, bottled water, and a tool kit to handle almost any situation that could arise, whether traveling to work, school, or across the country.

Most of us are a little bit of several of these, but we admit our preference is to be that Practical Prepper, the one who is most likely to bring common sense and level-headed thinking to the forefront. We prepare for the most likely threats we may face, but we realize that there exists the possibility of some type of financial, social, or civil collapse that may change life as we know it for some undetermined period of time. Still, we seek to maintain our cool heads regardless of the level of emergency we may face. Practical prepping significantly reduces the stress and anxiety that follows an emergency.

Chapter 2

Why Should You Be A Practical Prepper ?

The simple answer is STUFF HAPPENS! When it does, do you want to be prepared to handle it or be at the mercy of someone else?

Natural disasters happen. Do you want to be able to feed your family, keep them warm, dry, and happy for a few days or do you want to wait and hope someone brings food, water, and blankets?

In certain situations, if you don't already have what you need, it is too late to get it. Car insurance is a good example. If you don't have it when the wreck starts, it's too late. Same with seatbelts; if they aren't buckled when the wreck starts, it's too late. If a fire starts in the house, garage, or on the stove, it's too late to run to the local big-box store for a fire extinguisher. You have to be prepared *in advance*.

Do you wear your seat belt, have car insurance, use a smoke detector or have a fire extinguisher "just in case"? If so, you are already a prepper.

Do you buy toilet tissue one roll at a time, or do you purchase the 8-, 12-, or 24-roll pack? If you buy more than one roll at a time, and you are prepared for when the roll runs out, you are a prepper. (You can NEVER have too much quality toilet paper!)

How about jumper cables or a tool kit? If you have these, or even a membership to the Triple-A Auto Club, you are already a prepper.

When teaching disaster relief to volunteer organizations, our motto was, "Disasters Happen. Be ready." Being trained in disaster relief and having the basic tools, we were prepared to assist others when the need arose, and the need would arise, because disasters happen. In this context "Disasters happen. Be ready" means that you should have the basic necessities already on hand to get you through the event or at least until help eventually gets there.

Prepping gives you options.

Stuff happens. Be prepared. The everyday goal is to survive today, and wake up tomorrow. Astonishingly 45% of Americans have three days OR LESS food supplies in the house.

Why store food and water? Why have back-up heating? Why have basic tools to make repairs, jumper cables, and fix-a-flat? For the same reason you should have insurance, a fire extinguisher, and a smoke alarm. It is better to have it and not need it than to need it and not have it.

A side benefit of living a prepper lifestyle is, ultimately, you save money. You begin to look for bargains. Take advantage of BOGO (buy one, get one) sales, coupon shopping, or even buy in bulk. In addition, you save time, so when the daytrippers and panickers are rushing around from store to store looking for necessities, you can relax because you've stocked your prep spaces well ahead of an event.

Remember, the practical prepper is stocking up on items the family will actually eat or use, and rotates those items for freshness. You'll also have an "emergency supply" in case you run out of an item in your daily pantry. Krista will tell me she's "shopping the prepper pantry today". Just remember to replace what you use on your next regular grocery shopping trip.

Chapter 3

Making an emergency plan

Risk assessment

As discussed in chapter 3, the first step is to determine the threats you are most likely to face. The threat of natural disasters will be determined by the location in which you live. Here in the southeast, our threats are usually weather related. We live in tornado alley in north Alabama, so much of our preparing has to do with tornados. In the west and northwest, it is wild fires. On the Gulf and Atlantic coasts, hurricanes are a great threat.

When making an emergency plan, write down what will be needed during a particular event, what might cause you to have to leave your house, and where you would go. Include where your family members would meet if separated during the initial event.

Identify Hazards and Vulnerabilities

Some hazards you may identify may call for preparing to deal with that particular circumstance.

Hazards come in all types. Terrain, distance, heat and cold, potential attacks, or special needs could all be hazards needing to be addressed.

In some areas venomous snakes inhabit the woods and are often found near residences. If there is a possibility of needing to spend time in these areas, a pair of snake boots might be a good addition to the preps.

If there is a possibility of having to "bug out" because of fire or flood, can you transport enough food and water to be self-sustaining for several days?

Do you, or someone in your household have health issues that may restrict mobility? Can you transport that person safely from the area? How can you deal with this issue?

Are you in reasonably decent shape or do you need to get off the couch and get in shape. Many natural disasters require a lot of physical effort during recovery. Are you up to the task?

Identify Resources

After completing your risk assessment, identify the resources you have on hand, and resources you could attain for use if necessary.

You may not own a chain saw, but your neighbor may have one you could use. The same may apply to a tractor or a four-wheel drive vehicle, extension ladder, gas-powered water pump, or any other item.

You'll certainly want to be the good neighbor to others in need if you own items which will fill their need in a crisis.

Communications plan

Write out how you will receive information and emergency alerts. Local television stations do a good job of keeping viewers informed during weather events. What if you and your family are sleeping? You'll need a NOAA Weather Radio with Alert. Get one if you don't have one.

How will I let loved ones know of our condition after a disaster?

Write out the names, addresses, mobile numbers, and e-mail addresses of family members to contact. Remember, it may be much easier to get a text message through after a disaster than it is a voice call, as networks are usually overloaded, and text messages use much less bandwidth.

In our plan, we only have to make contact with one family member outside the impacted area and that family member will notify the others. We have that list in digital form as well as printed form, and have distributed the list accordingly.

How will you keep abreast of changing information and conditions and how will you contact others locally? A battery-operated radio is a must after a disaster to receive information. There are many good emergency radios on the market, offering multiple power options, including solar.

Two-way radios, such as ham radio, FRS, and GMRS radios give you the option of communicating with others in your local area. We cover this in detail in chapter 4, on communications.

Meeting Places

Your plan needs to include several meeting places in the event family members are separated after a disaster, or happen to not be at home at the time. One location should be nearby, such as at the end of the driveway, at a neighbors mailbox, or other easily identifiable location. In the event of a house fire or other calamity, it is much easier to determine that everyone is accounted for if there is a prearranged meeting location.

There needs to be a prearranged meeting location outside the neighborhood in case some members of the family are at work, at school, or simply away from home. This could be another family member's house, or similar location, as long as everyone knows where to meet if they are unable to return home.

Shelter Plan

Do you have a "safe room" or safe area in your home in case of severe weather threats? A storm shelter is best, but absent that a basement corner, basement room, windowless interior room on the lowest level, bathroom, or bathtub may be sufficient.

Will you be able to shelter in place, or will you have to leave your home? That depends on the threat. If you live in a low-lying area, it might be necessary to leave for higher ground. If you live in a mobile home, you absolutely need to seek safe shelter in a safer location. The largest percentage of fatalities during tornadoes comes from people refusing to leave the mobile home.

Many communities are putting up community shelters that will withstand extremely strong tornadoes and hurricanes. Many churches open shelters in their facilities during storms; many supported by the Red Cross and amateur radio operators.

If you can safely stay in place after a tornado, winter storm, or other natural disaster, what is your plan to stay warm (or cool), do you have enough food and water for the duration?

Shelter plan questions:

Will we shelter-in-place (Bug in)

Will we leave to seek shelter elsewhere? (Bug out)

Under what conditions will we leave? (Fire and flooding leaves no choice)

Meeting places in case we are separated

Evacuation Plan

What will make you leave for a longer period of time? Some friends on the south coast of Alabama, who grew up there, say that when a hurricane strengthens above a category two storm, they are already packed and ready to go, and won't wait until everyone else packs the highways trying to get out. It is easier and safer to leave early, even if it turns out to be just a family visit for a few days.

Special Needs Plan

Are there members of the family who have disabilities, special needs, medical needs, special dietary needs, pets, or other factors that may complicate getting through emergency situations or having to evacuate?

Is there anyone in the household with limited mobility? Would you need a wheelchair to move them away from the house? If you don't have one, do you know where you could get one or know of another means of moving them?

Address these needs, on paper, before the need arises. Have an ample supply of prescription medications to last not less than 10 days (thirty days preferred). Have extra pet food on hand, as well as a pet carrier. Most (but not all) short-term emergency storm shelters will accept pets if they are in a proper carrier.

Chapter 4

Getting Started

Brandon: *I'm independent. I don't like depending on someone else. I was a Boy Scout and learned the motto "be prepared."*

I have always carried a pocketknife and a flashlight. As a mechanic, if I had to borrow a tool the second time to do a job, I bought one to be prepared for the next time.

As a hiker, I prepared for multiple day backpacking trips. As the youngest beekeeper in my county, I have learned new skills that have provided our family with locally made honey and a little extra income from the sale of honey.

The first step in beginning your prepper journey is to do a threat assessment. That is, take a long look and make a list of the threats you are most likely to face, at your location, or in your situation.

Living in north and central Alabama, our greatest threats are weather-related. Alabama has more tornadoes than Oklahoma, and they're often devastating and deadly. Ice storms wreak havoc on power lines and trees. The rare snowfall can shut down a city for days (hey, it's the South). In the West and Northwest, wild fires cause evacuations. On the East and Gulf coasts, hurricanes are a regular occurrence. Most of these events cause extended power outages, sometimes lasting as long as a month in some areas. Normal food distribution systems are disrupted, cell phone and landline communications interrupted, and first responders risk their own safety to rescue others.

Other threats include economic downturns, corporate restructuring and down-sizing, resulting in job loss. Financial markets can collapse. Gasoline refining and delivery can be disrupted causing fuel shortages. Many things can be life-changing events, even if they are short-lived.

In 2019, the USA experienced a measles outbreak. Some locations were barring the presence of those who have not received the measles vaccine. Fortunately, it was limited to certain areas, but know that any virus could turn into a short-termed pandemic, causing schools, companies, and markets to shut down for a while. *How incredible that this very statement rang true in 2020 due to the global pandemic of COVID-19!*

Ask yourself, "What threats am I most likely to face?" Begin making preparations to be self-sufficient through those events.

Another threat we all face is injury around the house. You do have a decent first aid kit, don't you? Household-sized kits can be purchased ready-to-go, or you could assemble one yourself. Mini-kits are ideal for carrying in the car or a personal bag.

Automobile emergencies happen to people every day. The most common are flat tires, empty gas tanks, and dead batteries. Each of us can easily make preparations to handle these minor emergencies on our own.

After doing a threat assessment and determining the most likely events you could face, begin establishing your emergency plans and preps for each event. We know that most every plan includes the basics of food, water, shelter, and medicines, but you should consider the other items you'll need on hand as well as the possibility you will not be in your house when an emergency occurs. Be ready in your house, in your car, at work, or outdoors. Fill in the blanks:

"If _________________ happens, I will want or need
_________________."

A very good resource for beginning preppers is www.ready.gov. This website, administered by FEMA, has basic recommendations and is a great place to start. It recommends that everyone prepare to be self-sufficient for three days. Three days of food stores per person, three days of water stored at one gallon per day per person, and a three-day supply of toiletries, warm clothing, medications and other personal items. We'll see later that this is a starting point, not at all difficult to do, but, in some instances, not near enough.

A study of hurricanes Andrew (1992), Katrina (2005), and Maria (2017), indicated that it took an average of nine days for FEMA to get up and running in full swing for those individual events. Could you sleep outside for nine days waiting for shelter, food, clean water, medicines, or protection? What is your plan?

Some of us remember the "duck and cover" films presented by Burt The Turtle during the 1950s 'Cold War' as the country prepared for the possibility of nuclear attack. I'm not sure how much good being under a school desk and covering your head would do against a nuclear blast, but it was preparation and we did practice it.

One great program that came out of that same time period was "Grandma's Pantry." The film showed a youngster asking what Grandma had in the basket. She explained that it was "Grandma's Pantry," a *seven-day supply* of food and water to be used by the family in the event of a nuclear attack.

Burt The Turtle was written for children, and did a good job of relieving some of the fears American citizens faced at the time. As an aside, it also told the rest of the world that the United States was taking steps to survive any nuclear attack.

We find it interesting that the forerunner of FEMA recommended a seven-day emergency supply of food and water in the 1950s and 1960s, but now recommends a three-day supply. Our guess is that it was easier then to get people to take self-sufficiency more seriously than it is now. Considering 45% of Americans today have three days OR LESS of food in the house, it's at least a start. Besides, the Southern Baptist Disaster Relief teams and the Salvation Army usually set up big cooking trailers and Red Cross will deliver beans, chicken, and rice so those folks will have something to eat by day three.

After you have your three-day supply, work toward a seven-day supply, and eventually a one-month supply. This will prepare you for most natural disasters in North America. If you want to take things to the next level, establish a three-month supply. That would be very handy in the event of a job loss, severe economic downturn, or societal collapse.

Prepping In The Home

Let's get started.

First, and it should go without saying; you MUST have a fire extinguisher and a smoke detector in your home. You MUST.

Okay, it's time to start stocking up on food and water. Don't worry-- you don't have to buy it all at one time. If your budget is tight, you may need to take baby steps. The good news is that you can get started for less than five dollars.

Food Prepping

In this book, we are *not* going to be recommending buying a half ton of beans and rice, or a years supply of the twenty-five year storage freeze-dried foods. They have their place but they can be rather expensive. There is a better way of getting started.

The next time you buy groceries, buy two extra canned goods and a gallon of water. When you get home, set those aside as your first preps. Each time you buy groceries, buy two extra canned goods. If you buy groceries once per week, at the end of a year, you will have over a hundred cans of canned food. That could be approximately fifty meals for one, twenty-five meals for two, or over a dozen meals for a family of four. That's four days for four, over a week for two, and over two weeks for one. All this is done by buying only two extra cans per trip. Stock up a few gallons of water and you are off to a very good start. In fact, you will be well ahead of fifty percent of Americans when it comes to being prepared.

Buy and store foods your family will actually eat. It is no good storing food that your children refuse to eat. It is no fun eating food that is tasteless or totally bland, so include stores of spices and seasonings, such as salt, pepper, cinnamon, sugar, garlic and onion powders, BBQ rubs, oregano, and rosemary. It is also useless to store food that you will not be able to prepare. It is a good idea to write dates on the cans and boxes you store. This helps you rotate your food stores by using the FIFO method. FIFO is "first in, first out." This ensures that you always have fresh stock available without wasting food that may spoil over time.

Here's a list of some of the food items in our Prepper Pantry:

Assorted cans of beans, soups, tomato sauces, chili, ravioli, broths, vegetables and fruits

1-lb bags of long-grain rice

1-lb bags of dried beans

Canned hams, tuna, salmon, hash, chicken, BBQ, roast beef, stews

Ramen noodles, pasta, instant mac-n-cheese

Beef sticks, summer sausage, jerky

Crackers, cookies, chips, dips, spreadable cheeses

Ketchup, mustards, mayonnaise, grated dry Parmesan cheese

Worcestershire, soy, hot pepper, sweet n sour sauces

Dill pickles, sweet pickles, marinated mushrooms

Dry mixes, such as biscuit, cornbread, cakes, brownies, breads

Unsweetened applesauce and dry yeast for cake and bread leavening

Many of these foods can be eaten "as is" out of the package, no refrigeration or heat required. In the event of a prolonged power outage, I would use the gas grill on the patio (we keep small and large bottles of propane ready) for cooking and baking. Cast-iron or all-steel heavy cookware is best for grill use; refrain from using thin aluminum pots, or those with non-metal handles.

Krista: *"A few months ago, I came up with the idea to have "Prepper Supper", a meal built entirely out of what's in the prepper pantry, for two reasons: first, to rotate some of the items out, and second, to experience what eating "your plan" feels like. Providing for your family by prepping feels awfully good."*

Be sure to have several manual can openers on hand. The electric models are just paperweights if there is no electricity. Be sure to buy the good ones. The cheap ones don't stand up to long-term use, are harder to use, and break easily.

Water Storage

As vital as it is to collect and store non-perishable foods in our prepper pantries, our attention must focus on water storage first. Obviously, water is heavy and takes up a great deal more space than canned or vacuum-sealed foods, but water for consumption, hygiene, cooking, and cleaning puts it as our Number One commodity for practical prepping.

Most prepping manuals divide food/water supplies into three basic categories:

- Three-day (72-hour) emergency storage

- Three-weeks to three-months storage

- Longer-term storage, such as a year or more

Practical Preppers usually focus on the first two of these categories, but long-term water storage is great if you have the space to house it properly.

Three-day emergencies are generally the result of a severe storm or natural disaster, such as a tornado, hurricane, earthquake, or blizzard. It could take up to 72 hours for utilities to be fully restored after a cataclysmic event, and, in some cases, it takes much longer. Until then, many must shelter in place without electricity, plumbing, heat, air conditioning, and, in some cases, no cell phone or landline phone service either.

We've studied the advice of other preppers, and have learned from our own experience that large containers (5 or more gallons) are *not* practical for the three-day category. We advise you store bottled water in the pint-, liter-, and gallon-sized containers for the amount of drinking and cooking you may be doing during this time. We do not suggest you use up precious drinking water for bathing or hygiene purposes for an emergency of a few days; use baby cleansing wipes instead.

Calculate how much water you and your household will use for three days, then add 50% more to that amount. For example, We calculate the two of us would need 1.5 gallons *each* per day for drinking and cooking, so for a three-day event, we'd store 9 gallons total in an assortment of pints, liters, and gallons. In households with infants and/or elderly members, we suggest no less than a gallon each day for each of them.

Where and how you store your water requires some common-sense planning. Naturally, you want to be able to easily access your supplies when and if needed quick, fast, and in a hurry. Some homes have large attic spaces, but if the roof gets torn off in a storm, vital supplies might blow away with it. We'd recommend more practical choices:

• Pantry shelves	* Unused closets
• Underbed totes	* Pantry shelves
• Under staircases	* Large suitcases
• Heavy plastic solid crates	* Garages

- Backpack "go bags"   * Secured in cars

Water storage in the three- to six- month span is managed differently due to the larger quantities needed over a longer time frame. Some preppers will invest in UV-resistant blue containers of 5 gallons to dispense into smaller containers upon demand. Clean milk jugs are biodegradable, and disposable water bottles are too thin; *neither* of these is recommended for long-term storage. REMEMBER—water weighs 8.3 pounds per gallon, and long-term storage containers filled with water could weigh 50 pounds or more, so plan carefully when moving, filling, or storing water in these quantities.

For long-term water storage, use a BPA-free food-grade plastic barrel designed specifically for this purpose (*not* a rain barrel used at the downspout). The average capacity is 55 gallons, and it is highly recommended to use wood over the concrete to provide support underneath. One filled barrel could weigh as much as 500 pounds, so be careful how and where you place it, not just for safety, but also for access.

Stored water, in original unopened containers is still safe for use, although may have a stale taste when kept for many months. When Mark and I relocated to another city 100 miles away, we found some of our prepper gallons. They were close to two years in storage, so I chose to water plants with them instead. But, that experience caused me to be more mindful of rotating and replacing our water supply. We mark the date clearly in large magic marker for easy viewing on high shelves, with oldest dates to the front, newer to the back, for regular rotation.

If you must source your water from rainfall, ponds, creeks, rivers, lakes, or swimming pools, then you know you absolutely MUST purify it, either from chemical means, boiling, or with the use of a filtering straw device, such as a Lifestraw or Sawyer filter. Bacteria, pathogens, microbes, and parasites are no joke and could wreak havoc with your gut. Dehydration from vomiting or diarrhea could be life-threatening! Never take chances with your life and safety by consuming contaminated water, which can look muddy, murky, or crystal clear.

Chemical water purifiers:

- Liquid chlorine or chlorine tablets
- Iodine liquid or crystals
- Calcium hypochlorite powder and tablets

Liquid chlorine is measured at ¼ teaspoon for a gallon of contaminated water, or 4 drops per liter. Let stand 30 minutes before using. If using tablets, heat water first, add the tablets, let stand 30 minutes before using.

Tincture of iodine 2% is measured at 5 drops per quart of clear water, and 10 drops per quart of cloudy water. The crystal form is measured in capfuls per quart.

Calcium hypochlorite is usually found in 50-pound buckets and is typically used for much larger amounts of water.

SWIMMING POOL NOTE: pool owners may think, "My pool water is already treated with chlorine or polyhexamethylene biguanide. Why can't I just drink it straight? Safe, right?" It's safe for swimming in, but not intended for human or animal hydration. My own brother suffered illnesses for years associated with prolonged swallowing of pool water, chlorine poisoning. Avoid that by drinking it through a filtering straw or other filtering device to remove chlorine and bacteria.

Boiling water is appealing to those who do not wish to add chemicals to the water. If water is cloudy, allow time for the solids to collect at the bottom, pour it through a coffee filter or clean cloth into a pot, heat to a rolling boil for at least one minute. Let it cool completely before using.

Instant filtration "straws" are well-known among hikers and campers, and are a must for your "go bags". Some of these devices are rated for up to 100,000 gallons of use, and will filter out 99.9999% of all bacteria, such as salmonella, e. coli, and cholera, as well as 99.9999% of all protozoa, such as giardia and cryptosporidium. You fill a squeeze pouch with water, screw the filter onto the pouch, and either drink directly from the straw, or squeeze the filtered water into a bottle to share with others. This system is very practical and affordable.

If plain drinking water is unappealing to you on any ordinary day, you can add a fruit-flavored powdered mix or sugar-free option to make it more pleasant. Keep some of these flavoring supplements on hand in your water storage location.

NOTE: Tap water has already been treated with chlorine, so further treatment is not necessary. Some preppers still prefer to add 1/8 teaspoon chlorine per gallon anyway.

Staying Warm

Have extra warm blankets on hand in the event there is a power loss or the heat goes out. For extremely cold environments, you might wish to have sleeping bags for each person to sleep in, under the covers of their bed. An inexpensive one rated for around 50 degrees will suffice for most people, especially for short-term use of a few days.

For longer power outages, supplemental heat will likely be necessary. A fireplace can put out plenty of heat and you can move the family to the room where the fireplace is located. It might not be as comfortable as the bed, but sleeping on the floor, in a sleeping bag, near the fireplace would be mighty cozy.

In the late 1970s and early 1980s, the kerosene heater was the basic supplemental heat for many people, including us. Today, it is more likely to be a propane heater, just be sure that it is rated for indoor use, and have plenty of propane to last several days or weeks. Most of the small portable heaters use one pound propane bottles, but hoses are available to connect them to a twenty pound bottle (like those used for grills).

These hoses make using the heater more cost effective, and lasts a lot longer without having to change the bottle. Just be sure you have an ample supply on hand. We store some of the one pound bottles, as they are used on propane lanterns, and have a hose for the twenty pound bottles, as well as keeping a full twenty pound bottle at all times. It comes in handy when the grill bottle runs out half way through the grilling. Just don't forget to refill it and put it back on standby.

One possibility for staying warm without a fireplace is using one of the small portable heaters, rated for indoor use, and moving everyone to a smaller room rather than trying to heat large areas. The heater and sleeping bag would let you and your family sleep comfortably when the power or heat goes out.

Lights Out

It is important to be able to see when the lights go out. Otherwise, we wind up finding furniture with our little toes.

Some folks keep a "lights out kit" with flashlights, lanterns, batteries, candles and matches stored ready to go when things go dark.

We both carry flashlights in our EDC, and if one is not on us at the time, there is always one nearby in every room of the house. We have several small battery powered lanterns for lighting small areas, and a propane lantern for using outdoors, in the garage, and on the patio.

You can never have too many flashlights.

Be certain you have enough extra batteries in every size required by your flashlights.

Solar charged flashlights are great for having ready to use, if they are stored on a windowsill, especially in the window above the kitchen sink. The down side to a solar charged light is that when they do run out of power, they can't be recharged until daylight.

Basic Repairs

The practical prepper will be prepared for basic repairs around the house, which surely come to the average homeowner or renter. These emergencies seem to happen when the big box stores are closed, so you need to consider having materials for basic repairs on hand at all times. We keep the items necessary to repair a leaky toilet or leaky faucet on hand at all times. Water leaks are another possibility, and pinhole leaks can be repaired with a piece of rubber and a hose clamp. At least have the tools necessary to shut off the water in the event of a major water leak. This can be done with an adjustable wrench, or even a pair of vice grips.

Everyone should have basic hand tools available, such as screwdrivers, adjustable wrenches, pliers, hammer, electrical tape, shovel, and a few others.

A ladder, tarp, and nails can make temporary repairs to the storm-damaged roof, or cover windows destroyed by flying debris.

Prepping With Children

We have two new grandchildren, and we are aware how many diapers they can go through, how much formula they can consume, and how many baby items are necessary to keep those precious little ones healthy and happy.

If you have small children, be sure to store enough diapers and formula to make it seven days or more without restocking. Rotate these quickly so that you always have the correct size and fresh formula available.

The same goes for baby food for children not yet eating table food. Snacks and comfort food is great for small children when the power goes out.

Keep age appropriate games on hand as well as books to keep them occupied during this time. Too many children are addicted to "devices" and on-line games. They will quickly get bored and experience withdrawals from the electronic life. Be prepared to occupy their minds, or YOU may lose your mind.

Prepping for Pets and Livestock

Don't forget about preparing for your pets as well. Store an extra supply of food and water for them, just as you do for yourself and your family. Maintain the exact same foods for your pet during an emergency—a sudden switch to 'people food' could really cause a digestive nightmare for them, and you!

Since dogs are considered "man's best friend", shouldn't we include our pets in any emergency plan? Naturally, in our efforts to prep, stock, and store our own food, water, and shelter necessities, we must also do the same equally for our beloved dogs, cats, birds, fish, hamsters, rabbits, guinea pigs, hermit crabs, turtles, lizards, and snakes, or the "farm" groups of animals, such as chickens, turkeys, ducks, goats, sheep, cows, horses, alpacas, llamas, emus, and ostriches. My apologies if I've inadvertently omitted your pet in this list; you get my point anyhow.

Pet owners/caregivers usually know well how much and what types of food their pets consume daily, weekly, or monthly, and also the quantities of water required each day. If we are storing food and water for ourselves for a week, then logic dictates we store our pet's requirements for the same time period.

Here are some money-saving pet food "hacks" you can use now when there's no emergency, but may help get you started on pet prep:

* Purchase dry food in the largest available bag, then portion out several amounts in ziploc bags to store in the

freezer. Take out what you need, then store the rest long-term.

* Call the customer service departments of pet food brands asking them for coupons. They're more than happy to send you several!

* Ask your local pet specialty store if they have a loyalty program for pet food purchases, like, get a free bag when you buy 10, etc. Free bag = free prep!

Most pets only hydrate with water, unlike us humans, who drink all sorts of beverages, so take that into account when you store water for them.

Tropical fish can survive several days, even weeks, without benefit of aquarium heaters or filters, but you must cut back on your feeding and cleaning routine. In a heated aquarium, the loss of power means a gradual drop in temperature, to which many species can adjust. Have some "vacation feeder" blocks on hand to supplement them over time, and do NOT empty the entire tank of its old water (shouldn't do that anyway). Make 10%-20% water changes if power is out for 7 or more days; otherwise, don't fret about how murky the water looks in the tank, because fish can live in slimy, cloudy waters all over the world with no problem.

Reptiles, by nature, must have some warm area in which to bask periodically during the day, and natural sunlight works well for that, but let me caution you about that; hauling a 30-gallon reptarium out into 12 hours of skin-searing summer sun is certain death for your scaly sweetie. Once a reptile has warmed sufficiently for blood flow and digestive purposes, it will seek dark hiding spots for the remainder of the day. Unless you have your own cricket or mealworm habitat for long-term feeds, train your snake or lizard to eat frozen prey or pelleted foods in case your live prey source is no more. If you find a mouse, cricket, or grasshopper in the wild, offer that as food, if you wish.

Parasite control is on the prep list, both the internal types (hookworm, roundworm, tapeworm, giardia, and coccidia, etc.), and external types (scabies, fleas, ticks, mange). Plus, if your pet is on some sort of prescribed protocol for conditions like diabetes, epilepsy, intestinal disorders, or prolonged eye/ear treatments, you should discuss your concern with your pet's doctor and inquire about the most reasonable and effective forms of medications that you can provide in case you're snowed-in, cannot drive, or have "bugged out".

For those of you who care for livestock found on farms, you're already prepping in meaningful ways for your animals with their food, water, and shelter requirements. Most farms have deep wells as a water source, but are usually pumped electrically, so have a plan of action for water when the power goes down. Farmers are better prepared than most for long-term animal care, evidenced by huge barn lofts filled with hay and straw, silos filled with grain, and acres of crops to refill these spaces when needed.

Ok, nobody likes to discuss his or her waste management plan, but we HAVE to have one, of course. Well, so does your pet. Your homework assignment is to imagine several scenarios where you and your pet(s) are "marooned" without electrical power; that automatic litter box won't scoop itself now! Will your cat have enough fresh clumping litter? Will your dog have access to grass outside for its "business"? Rabbit and guinea pig litter can pile up quickly--what's your discard plan for that? (Think "compost").

Finally, but most importantly, focus on this: pets are ours to love and care for 100%, and they give more to us than they'd ever take. We owe them no less care than we owe our children, and even scientists have measured pets' abilities to calm us, care about us, listen to and love us, and provide much-needed companionship at a level of devotion that's rich and rare. How many times have we read or heard the story of a lost dog traveling hundreds of miles to reunite with its family, or how therapy pets help folks regain their speech or movement skills? How many people survived an emergency situation because their pet was nearby? How important is your pet to YOU?

Other Considerations At Home

Ladies, don't forget to prep in the area of feminine products. From what I understand, there is no convenient alternative to the store bought items, so stock up. They don't go bad, and even if you no longer need them, they will be great for barter in the event of a long-term event.

Basic hygiene is a concern for the practical prepper.

Have a supply of toilet paper on hand. Things can be used as a substitute, but none are as good as that which is designed for that job. It only makes sense to keep a good supply on hand.

The water usually flows and the toilet flushes in most power outages, but both will stop if the power outage is widespread enough and long enough to cause the water system's pumps to quit operating. Stored water can be used for drinking, cooking, and washing. Toilets can be flushed with water from a bucket. You can fill the back of the toilet and store it there until the next flush, or you can flush by pouring the water directly into the bowl.

Chapter 5

Storing Supplies

Supplies are items you can eat, drink, or with which you can solve a problem. This includes food, water, flashlights, batteries, tools, tarps, knives, and all your other "preps."

Over time, supplies can add up to a lot of items to be stored. Some of your preps may not be affected by temperature changes and therefore able to be stored in a garage or out buildings. Items such as hand tools, tarps, wood, nails, and such can be stored without concern that they may get too hot or too cold. Other items need to be in controlled climate storage. Food, water, and medications fall into this category.

Consideration must also be given to keeping your preps free from rodents. Rats, mice, and squirrels love to get into paper products, and will chew through cardboard boxes and even plastic to get to your preps. Therefore, they should be stored in a way to keep rodents away, or checked regularly to protect the integrity of the storage containers.

Squirrels love to come in through gaps between to roof and rafters, and will even chew out an area to get through. Mice will do the same around doors, and where pipes go through walls. Steel wool can be stuffed into the holes to help keep the little devils out, or pest control products can be used to keep them at bay. We are looking for a couple of plastic owls or hawks to put in the garage rafters to see if that has any effect.

Our kitchen cabinets have small cabinets above the normal storage areas. This makes a great place to store food preps. A closet can be shelved giving a fair amount of storage space. Food may be stored in flat containers and stored under beds. We lived in an apartment when we first married. We found that under-bed storage and a round table with a floor-length tablecloth gave us storage space for a fair amount of supplies.

Vehicle storage is determined by what you drive; a pick-up truck with a toolbox could carry a chainsaw, fire-axe, thirty feet of logging chain, a come-along, tent, tarp, sleeping bag, camp stove and cookware, but if you drive a mini smart car, your space will be somewhat limited.

There are compartments and locations in most vehicles where small items can be stored out of sight. On top of and around the spare tire, usually stored under the trunk flooring, can provide out-of-the-way storage for jumper cables, small hand tools, or even a tow strap.

Chapter 6

Prepping In The Automobile

Your Everyday Vehicle

Mark: *"For years I kept a set of jumper cable hanging in the basement before it dawned on me that if they were in the car and I needed them at home, I could get them out of the car. If they were hanging in the basement and I needed them away from home, I didn't have them. They have been riding in the car since. The cost of that prep was moving an item I already owned. I did the same with hand tools, creating a mall bag to be kept in each vehicle"*

With a few items you can find in the garage, at the dollar store, discount store, or thrift store (the serious preppers supply store) you can have your car ready to handle most of the emergencies we face in our daily travels.

Pliers, an adjustable wrench, screwdrivers, duct tape, electrical tape, and spare fuses sure come in handy at times. These can be picked up for very little investment at a big box store, automotive store, and for nearly nothing at a pawnshop. These can be kept in a small bag in the trunk, under a seat, or even on top of the spare tire. They are out of the way, but always there if needed.

If you have the skill to plug a flat tire (not hard) a tubeless tire plug kit costs a few bucks at the big box discount store. A barley used 12-volt air compressor can be found for five bucks or so at the thrift store. Almost anyone can use a can of Fix-a-flat" in an emergency, and those are just a few bucks as well. (Be sure to tell the tire repair location that you had to use 'fix-a-flat." Make sure they clean it out. Long-term exposure to the chemicals can cause damage to your tire, but it sure comes in handy when you need it).

Add a one-gallon gas can (tightly sealed) and a gallon of gas and you can handle the top three automobile emergencies most people will face.

It is also a good idea to not let your fuel tank get below a half tank, especially in the winter.

Krista: *"I made the trip from Alabama to North Carolina to be there when my newest grandson was born. What is normally an eight-hour trip including rest stops food and gas took fifteen hours. Six hours of that was sitting on a bridge waiting for a wrecked tanker truck to be cleared. I was about twenty-five miles from where we usually stop for fuel, and yes, we tended to run it down to a little under a quarter tank of fuel in order to save an extra stop. Well, you can use a quarter tank of fuel sitting in the cold for six hours. It was close, but I was able to get fuel just in time. That tightly sealed one gallon can of gas that now rides along on all trips sure would have been comforting that night."*

Other items you may want to add to your vehicle are an even larger tool kit, blanket or sleeping bag (indoor use, 40-50 degree rated), a four-way lug wrench, and a tire pressure gauge. We'll share more later on what we call our "go bags" that "go where we go." These give you a lot more options when away from home, and come in very handy on a regular basis.

That's how easy it is to start being a practical prepper. You'll want to add more things as time goes along or as you think of things you might need after a disaster or in an emergency, and we promise that we'll help you think of a lot more. Sometimes all that will be needed is rounding up things you have and putting them in an easily accessible place. You'll be a practical prepper; no bunker needed.

Prepping Off-road Vehicles

The avid off-roader is well acquainted with not only the joys of off-roading, but also the perils and predicaments in which they can find themselves. All off-road vehicles should have a supply of food and water aboard, and here are a few more items that should be carried if possible.

An axe or machete comes in handy when the vehicle slides into a location where there is a small tree between the bumper and the body of the vehicle.

A folding shovel works wonders when all four tires are sitting off the ground spinning because you slid off into the ruts and both 'chunks' are sitting on dirt.

A winch, or come-along and cable, will help when you slide two tires off the side of the road and can't get out on your own.

A tow strap or cable comes in handy when your fuel pump goes out seven miles from civilization (if you have a buddy to pull you out).

All the above are from personal experience. Thankfully, the four-wheel drive was properly prepared.

Additionally, it is a good idea to carry a tool kit, duck take, several flashlights, and rope in the vehicle. They all can come in mighty handy at times. A small fishing kit can provide some fun as well as a good meal when you come upon that hidden lake or stream that is so out of the way it almost never gets fished.

Chapter 7

Communications

Communications is simply a way of sending and/or receiving information. It can be two people sitting in the same room having a conversation, or it can be two HAM radio operators half a continent apart. If information is being exchanged, communication is taking place.

Two older ladies lived across the street from each other. They had a system of checking on each other every morning. The agreement was that when they got up each morning, they raised a particular window shade. Each would look out to see that the shade was raised by a certain time each morning, and if not the other was to send help. It was a very simple system for them, but it worked.

An unknown quote: "If I cannot communicate with you after the SHTF, you are just someone I used to know." That is just how important communications are, so let's get started.

Communications can be divided into two categories: one-way, and two-way.

One-way communications can be commercial broadcast radio and television, NOAA-weather radios, short-wave radios, emergency-survival radios, or any other means used to receive information.

Two-way communications is capable of sending and receiving information. Cell phones, walkie-talkies, social media, text messaging, email, CB radio, and amateur (HAM) radio are effective methods of two-way communications. Our two ladies above were also using very effective two-way communications. Each method has its merits and limitations.

After a devastating storm event, the electricity may be out, cell phones likely won't work, and landline systems will overload quickly, and could be inoperable for hours or days, so how can word get out that you're okay or your loved ones are okay? You may need to rely on other forms of communication.

Let's begin with one-way communications; receiving information. It is essential that we have a way of receiving information during major emergency events

One-way Communications

Weather Radios

One radio that should be in every home across the nation is a NOAA weather radio with alert tones. These radios are programmable to your county or area. They operate on household current as well as battery backup, and will alert whenever the National Weather Service puts out a warning, watch, or other alert. These alerts will wake you if you are sleeping and give you time to take action. That action might be turning on the television to see what the meteorologist is saying, or it might be getting into a safe room or storm shelter. These radios save lives! If you do not have one stop reading, go to the store now, and buy one. That is how important having one really is.

We have the First Alert WX-150. On this radio, the types of alerts you receive are selectable, and tornado warnings cannot be disabled, but others can. On our weather radio, we have tornado warnings, thunderstorm warnings, and amber alerts enabled. All of our watch alerts are disabled. Being weather nerds, we already have information on the watches in the area, and where we live avalanche and high sea alerts are not applicable. The WX-150 is just a NOAA weather radio, but it serves our purpose very well.

Another radio with which we are impressed is the Kaito KA-500. This radio has multiple ways to charge making it a great radio for short or long duration power outages. It has an internal rechargeable NiMH battery pack, can be operated with a wall plug charger, three AA batteries, a solar panel, dynamo hand crank, and can be charged through a USB input.

The Kaito KA-500 has a reading lamp on the back of the solar panel, receives AM, FM, two short-wave bands, and all seven NOAA weather frequencies. It can also charge other devices such as cell phones, tablets, or any devise using a 5 volt USB cable charger.

Though not as popular today with the ability to watch television on smart phones, tablet, and computers, the old-fashioned battery operated television has a place during power outages. Not only can they provide needed information, they can be a source of entertainment during extended power outages.

Mark: *During the 'blizzard of '93" in central Alabama our house was without power for seven days and nights. Each night, with nothing but kerosene lamp for lighting, we watched the nightly movie at the kitchen table on a battery operated five inch black and white television.*

The Weather Channel and cable news channels are great for keeping up with what is going on around the country, but when it comes to local weather situations, you need a way to receive local weather information.

There are smart phone apps that provide weather warnings. There are local sources that provide text messages and e-mail messages with weather alerts. And of course, there are the outdoor weather sirens incase you are outside at the time, but don't depend on these inside unless you live within a block or two of a siren.

In many circles, there is a saying, "Two is one, and one is none." The idea is that you have a back up. When you have two of something and one fails, you have a backup. If you have only one and it fails, you have none. Have multiple ways to receive weather alerts

Two -way Communications

Cell Phones

The most widely used form of two-way communication available today is the cell phone.

Important Note: Federal law requires that all cell phones be able to dial 911 if they can be powered up, regardless of whether or not they are connected to a carrier. I've often recommended that people without a cell phone obtain an unused phone, keep it charged, and carry it with them, on their person, in case of emergency, and keep it by the bedside at night. It will dial 911 only, so be sure that it's truly an emergency or serious matter. This is especially useful for shut-ins who use a landline phone, in case the landline goes out. It is also advisable that those living alone, who do not have some type of "Life Alert" system, carry the phone on them in case of a fall. Without having to try to get to the landline, they can simply pull out the "911-only" cell phone and call for help.

A similar situation occurred with a family member recently. She fell, broke bones and was unable to get up. Having her cell phone on her person allowed her to summon help from a family member a few blocks away, and she called 911 to get medical help on the way.

Sometimes, cell phone traffic becomes overloaded or inoperable, as is often the case after a tornado. If that happens, try text messaging. Text messages use much less bandwidth than voice or video calls, and you may find that you are able to communicate via text when it is nearly impossible to complete a voice call.

This was certainly the case for our family during the April 27, 2011 tornadoes that passed through Alabama, taking 353 lives. We were in a shelter in Riverside, Alabama, manning the HAM radio and watching every source of weather information available to us, including GRLevel 3® radar from Gibson Ridge® – weather nerds really need to check this one out; there's a fully operational free trial. www.grlevelx.com

We watched as the EF-4 tornado tracked across an area about 40 miles away, an area where two of our daughters and their families lived at the time.

It was 20 minutes before they were able to get a text message to us letting us know they were safe. It took another two hours before a voice call was completed.

On that night, one son-in-law decided he would obtain his amateur radio license so we would be able to communicate almost instantly, if ever again put in that situation. Twenty minutes is a LONG time to wait to hear your family is safe.

Satellite Phones

There are numerous satellite communications companies providing voice and data communications from anywhere on the earth. Depending on the service package, prices range from around $5.00 per minute to $16.00 per minute, at the time of this writing. The equipment is expensive, at a thousand dollars or more, per unit, and subscriptions are required. They have their place and purpose, and could be a consideration for some.

Have A Way To Recharge Your Devices

All communications devices require power. Without power, they become useless. For that reason, the practical prepper will be prepared for power outages and have a way to recharge their phones and other devices.

There are many systems available commercially that are both portable and powerful. A quick internet search revealed many powerful and affordable options, price depending on amount of power being stored. There are inexpensive pocket sized options in the $10-$15 range capable of recharging many phones once ad well as larger versions capable of charging powerful energy hog devices multiple times. There are portable chargers available with not only USB ports, but also USB-C ports and A/C ports for recharging laptops.

During an extended power outage, other items may be a source of power for your devices. A UPS - uninterruptible power supply used by many on desktop computers is a ready source, just plug in the wall charger and charge your phone.

Many amateur radio operators maintain a 12 volt car battery and trickle charger to power mobile radios in their radio rooms, or "ham shack." The same idea can be used with either a cigarette lighter plug receptacle or power inverter attached. With an inverter attached, many other devices needing household current can be used as well. Don't expect to be able to run the refrigerator off of a car battery and inverter, but depending on the size of the inverter, many useful items could be utilized. Small fans, box fans, radios, televisions, satellite receiver, lamps, rechargeable battery chargers, cell phone chargers, and computer equipment come to mind. Keep in mind that the car battery has a limited supply of electricity available that can be depleted with heavy use. However, it is possible to recharge the car battery by putting it back into the vehicle and allowing the engine to run for a while. For a longer battery life and the ability to recharge the battery more times, a marine deep-cycle battery or RV battery can be used.

Radio Communications

A little understanding is necessary when considering radio use for prepper communications, but we'll keep it simple for the purposes of this book. There are many good resources if you would like to develop an in-depth working knowledge of radio theory, operations, and the opportunities for involvement in amateur radio operations. For example, www.arrl.org is a great place to start for learning the basics of amateur radio.

The radio operations we will feature in this book are divided into three basic categories, or bands: HF (High Frequency), VHF (Very High Frequency), and UHF (Ultra High Frequency). Radio frequencies referenced in this book are measured in megahertz (MHz)

The actual frequencies are:

o HF: 3 MHz - 30 MHz or 100 meters - 10 meters
o VHF: 30 MHz - 300 MHz or 10 meters - 1 meter
o UHF: 300Hz – 3 GHz (gigahertz)

HF is used for short-wave radio, some aviation communications, government time stations, amateur radio, and citizens band communications, among others. Radio waves in this band can be bounced back to earth by the ionosphere, allowing very long range, even worldwide communications.

VHF is used for more local communications, the distance of which can be increased by height, antenna gain, and directional antennas. VHF is often used by FM radio broadcasting, television, and marine and land mobile radio stations i.e., some public service, police departments, fire departments, and emergency medical services, amateur radio, FRS and GMRS services, as well as aircraft ground and airborne operations. VHF is primarily "line of sight" communications, but does work reasonably well in mountainous areas.

UHF is used for television broadcasting, GPS, personal radio services, some cordless phones, Wi-Fi, Bluetooth, walkie-talkies and many other applications. UHF is primarily "line of sight" communications. Hills, mountains, and large buildings can block the signal, reducing the effective distance. It does seem to work well through interior walls, making it great for indoor operation.

Two Way Radio Communications

Two-way radio systems usually operate in a half-duplex mode. Unlike full duplex systems such as telephones, where both parties can talk and hear simultaneously, half-duplex systems are either/or. You can either transmit or receive. One party presses the transmit button while the other listens, and then the roles are reversed.

Simplex Operation

Simplex operation utilizes one frequency to both transmit and receive. It is used radio to radio, and is limited in the distance over which the radios may communicate.

Simplex operation may be utilized anywhere two radios are set to the same frequency and the radios are within range, and that range may be decreased depending on terrain, buildings, or large obstacles.

We have used radios on simplex frequencies while hunting, fishing, and even with family spread out in the mall or at an event, both on the amateur radio bands as well as the Family Radio Services, depending on whether or not the other radio operator held a current amateur radio license.

Repeater Operation

In repeater operations the radios utilize two frequencies and a repeater. The simple explanation is that the radios transmit on the frequency that the repeater receives, and the repeater simultaneously retransmits on the frequency that is received by the radios.

Repeater frequencies must be pre-programmed into your radio, along with any required privacy tones (PL Tones) before the repeater may be used. Repeater programming can be done from the keypad or microphone on most hand held and mobile radios, but most of us find it much easier to program from the computer.

Radio Services

Let's talk about some of the radio services available that may be used:

Family Radio Service

The Family Radio Service (FRS) is a two-way, short-distance communications service authorized by the FCC in 1996. It's designed to accommodate family and group short-range communication needs using small handheld radios.

The FRS utilizes 22 channelized frequencies in the 462 MHz and 467 MHz range. An individual license is not required, there's no minimum age requirement, and it may be used for personal or business reasons, as long as you comply with the rules.

FRS channels 1-7 and 15-22 may utilize up to two watts of power, and channels 8-14 are limited to one-half watt. Later, we will provide a list of channels advertised on some forums where different groups can be found after an SHTF event.

General Mobile Radio Service

The GMRS is comprised of thirty channelized frequencies in the 462 MHz and 467 MHz range (UHF). Yes, it's the same frequency range as the FRS, but they are interspersed between the FRS frequencies. The FCC allows repeater use on some of the GMRS channels as well as limited data applications, such as text messaging across the system.

The General Mobile Radio Service (GMRS) requires an FCC license (good for ten years) according to Rule Part 47 C.F.R. part 95 subpart E. You may apply for a license if you are 18 years of age or older, but any family member regardless of age, may operate the radio under that license.

The radios often purchased at sporting goods and big-box stores, and labeled as "26 mile radios", are usually in the FRS and/or GMRS bands. Don't count on that "26 miles" unless you happen to be at sea, climb the sailing mast, and make contact with someone else at the top of his or her mast 26 miles away. They are good, though, for that which they are designed: short-range family or group communications, and they certainly have a place in communications after a disaster or SHTF situation.

Imagine if your entire neighborhood had these radios, all set to the same channel, and ready to use during and after disasters. Trapped survivors might be located and rescued sooner, the injured located and attended more rapidly, or the rest of the neighborhood informed of hazards in a more timely fashion.

Multi-Use Radio Service

The Multi-Use Radio Service (MURS) is comprised of five channelized frequencies in the 151-154 MHz range (VHF). MURS transmissions are limited to a maximum of two watts of power output. Range of these radios is limited to a short-range distance of about two miles, but an external antenna can extend that range out to as much as ten miles. We have used the MURS while traveling in a group, and with the use of magnetic VHF antennas, and we have experienced solid communications out to seven miles on the road.

The MURS does not require an individual license, and there is no age restriction on operating on the MURS band.

Amateur Radio

Amateur Radio just may be the absolute best radio communications system available for communications during and after any disaster or SHTF situation. Local disaster organization such as ARES (Amateur Radio Emergency Services) as well as individual operators WILL be on the air during and after local severe weather situations, tornadoes, hurricanes, or man-made disasters. Many will deploy to provide coordinated communications from shelters, Emergency Management Operations Centers, (EMA EOC), Red Cross and

Salvation Army centers, command posts, and sometimes in search and rescue (SAR) operations.

Amateur radio (HAM radio) operators have been instrumental in helping to locate missing children, dementia patients, elderly people, as well as providing essential communications into and out of severely damaged disaster areas where all other communications have been lost. When all else fails, HAM radio WORKS!

Amateur Radio encompasses many modes of communication ranging from old-school Morse Code, (referred to as CW or continuous wave), to satellite communications, voice communications, telegraphy, even television transmissions via HAM radio across twenty-seven frequency bands.

Some bands are used for local communication through simplex (single frequency), or by using repeaters. Mobile radios operate with as much as 80 watts, base stations with amplifiers up to 1500 watts on some bands, and handheld radios operating at 8 watts are now available. Other bands can accommodate worldwide and inter-continental communications on HF.

Mark: *Eighty meters is a band where regular communications across several states can be found. One night, in the central Alabama woods, in a camper with my son-in-law, using a mobile radio (Yaesu 857D) powered off a car battery under the table, and a very temporary 14 gauge wire strung across two trees, I participated in a "rag chew" with folks in Florida, North Carolina, Mississippi, and Texas, with a few others around the country popping in at times.*

A license is required, and there are currently three licenses available, and each requires a test. Morse Code is no longer required for any license class, but it is still alive and well on HAM radio, and can establish contact when other means fail.

The Technician Class license is the first level license available. The Technician test isn't very hard, if you study a bit, and study guides and practice tests are available online for all classes.

HAMTESTONLINE.COM® is an online resource which, for a fee, provides study material on each subject, provides explanations and helpful hints to remember correct answers, and provides practice tests. At the time of this writing, the listed price for the technician class study course is $24.95, which includes a 100% money back guarantee.

Study guide books may be purchased for each license class, and the question pool from which test questions are selected may be downloaded in printable form from the American Radio Relay League (ARRL) website at www.arrl.org at no cost.

If you elect to go with purchasing study guides, QRZ.com® is a site that provides practice tests at no cost, and has helped many amateur radio operators pass the tests.

Krista: *I bought the ARRL Technician Study Guide on Wednesday and began studying. I was off the rest of the week, so I kept studying. On Thursday night, I began taking (and failing) practice tests on www.QRZ.com. On Friday, I started passing tests, getting even higher scores over the weekend, and passed the license test on Monday night. Now I am KN4CMT.*

Technician class operators are licensed to operate on all frequencies in the amateur bands 50 MHz and above, and have limited privileges in the ten-meter band (28.300 – 28.500), which at times allows worldwide contacts to be made.

This license class covers the two-meter (144.00 - 148.00 VHF) and the seventy-centimeter (420.00 –

450.00 UHF) bands, where most local and repeater communications take place. The majority of new 'Technicians' begin on the two-meter band, make local contacts, make new friends, and even get involved in any number of activities involving HAM radio. Activities include amateur radio clubs, ARES (Amateur Radio Emergency Services), SKYWARN (weather spotting), public service events, providing communications for marathons, bike rides, and even endurance horse rides through national forests where cell phones are not reliable. Many search-and-rescue (SAR) teams and disaster relief teams are composed of HAM radio volunteers, or have at least one (referred to as a 'communicator') on the team.

Here's a good illustration for you. Each year, in the spring, a group of HAM radio friends camp in the east Alabama woods of the Talladega National Forest providing communications for the Yellowhammer Endurance Horse Ride.

Twelve checkpoints, throughout the trail route and a base station located at the ride command center (fancy term for under a tent in the stable area) are manned by HAM radio operators and unlicensed volunteers, as riders compete in a three-day event involving 75-mile, 50-mile, and 25-mile events. (We can't imagine riding 75 miles in a day on a HORSE, but these folks do it in an area where cell phones are useful ONLY if you drive to the top of the nearest mountain, stand on the back of the truck with one arm and one leg raised, and then you might get a cell signal, if you don't fall off the truck).

You can be assured these operators protect lives! Even with the long hours, cold winds, and sleeping in a tent or camper, these operators have the time of their lives and wouldn't be anywhere else on that weekend, if at all possible We were planning to be there with them this year, but the event has been cancelled due to the COVID-19 crisis, but we'll be there next year.

Mark: *I have participated in most of the above activities across my years as a licensed amateur radio operator, and have seen the presence of a HAM radio operator lead to the saving of a life, in getting timely emergency medical assistance, even in the middle of nowhere. Both licensed and unlicensed volunteers are welcome at most of these events, and your assistance will be greatly appreciated, and you will find many of these events to be personally rewarding.*

General and Extra Class licenses open up a lot more band space in which to operate, especially in the HF bands. General and Extra class license holders may operate in the lower bands, even down to 3.4 MHz (80 meters) and 1.8 MHz (160 meters) which, at times, provide world-wide communications, including Antarctica.

The difference in General and Extra Classes on an operational level is that Extra class has a little more operating space across some bands. Both classes can do the exact same thing, with the Extra Class Operator being able to do it in a little more band space.

I would recommend anyone interested in communicating after a large impact area, communications-interrupting disaster, SHTF situation, or anyone just wanting to talk across the nation or internationally, study and obtain at least a General Class license.

If you get your ham license and a UHF/VHF radio, check out the local training "nets" available in your area. Local amateur radio club websites will give you the day, time, and repeater on which the nets are held.

The nets are 'directed' and the net operator will tell you when you should check in with your call sign, first name, and location. This is the format used during emergencies and the information lets the net operator to call for more information (usually weather observations) from a particular area. The nets are a great way to get used to talking on your radio, and it is fun.

CB Radio

The FCC created the Citizen Band Radio Service, or CB for short, in 1945. It is a form of radio intended to be used for short range communications, can be used for personal or business use, and no longer requires a license.

Though CB radio should not be considered a viable replacement for amateur (Ham) radio, the radios do have their place, and should be a part of the communications preps for survivalists and preppers.

Even though CB radio reached its peak of popularity in the 1970s, there are many people who still use CB as a hobby. It is also used by members of hunting and fishing clubs, and cross-country travelers.

Most truck drivers use CB radios to share updates on weather conditions, traffic conditions, detours, and even the locations of police running radar.

Depending on the antenna, mobile and handheld CB radios are usually limited to four or five miles under normal conditions, at the legal power limit of four watts.

The CB radio frequency spectrum is divided into forty channels and may be used in AM mode and USB (upper side band) mode. The most commonly monitored channels are the emergency channel 9 (27.065 MHz) and the channel most used by truckers and travelers is channel 19 (27.185 MHz).

If your activities are limited to areas within about five miles of the interstate system, a CB radio may be a viable means of communicating during an emergency situation, though it might require that you get to the top of a hill to contact passing motorists. CB radios can be useful in disaster impact areas as normal cell service is often interrupted when cell towers are damaged or overloaded. CB radios would be excellent in communicating with neighbors within a small community or sub-division, and could be used not only during emergency situations, but also for community events.

For preppers, CB radio is just another tool in the toolbox, to be utilized in their communications plan.

"Talking" On A Radio During Emergencies

In the event you do have to use your radio for emergency communications, it is best to use "plain language" while communicating. That means NO "10 codes," "Q-signals" or "good-buddy" language. Be clear, concise, and to the point – USE PLAIN LANGUAGE, and use clean language.

Mobile Radios

The handheld radio is the lightest, most portable radio you can have, and it is highly recommended that you have at least one, if not several, in your arsenal of communication tools.

However, there are times when you may need more than a handheld radio to establish communications; hence, the mobile radio.

Mobile radios operate on 12 volts, and may be mounted in a vehicle, operated anywhere using a 12-volt battery, or with commercial power utilizing a 12-volt power supply.

Mobile radios are available which operate with as little as 0.5 watts, or as much as 100 watts. There are single-band radios and some are multi-band radios. Some mobile radios cover HF, VHF, and UHF. Many HAM operators utilize a mobile radio and power supply as their primary "base" radio.

We personally have a Yaesu® 857D multi-band radio and a 25-amp 12-volt power supply set up in our office/radio room. This combination has served us well. It has been taken it into the woods and operated on a 12-volt car battery, as well as carried half way across the country and operated with a 12-volt "jump box" designed for jumping a car with a dead battery. This radio has been used from the office, truck, and the woods to make hundreds of contacts around the world.

The mobile is worthy of consideration especially if you take your vehicle into areas off the beaten path, camping, hunting, fishing, four wheeling, or anywhere else where you may not have reliable cell service.

Antennas

A friend once told me that a thousand dollar radio and a ten dollar antenna is a ten dollar system, and that a one-hundred dollar radio with a hundred-dollar antenna will out talk it any day. I have found that to be pretty much a universal truth across the board. Do not cut corners on your antenna. You WILL regret it.

There are as many antenna options as there are radios available. The worth of many is questionable, especially when used across any kind of distance. We'll limit this section to those that may be used as portable, mobile, or in the backcountry. Let's consider a few:

The "Rubber-Duck" antenna, which comes with most handheld radios, is a fantastic little antenna when used in the back yard as the grandsons play "Army" or when you need to communicate over a limited distance. In my experience, the "rubber-duck" is good for a few miles when using a repeater, and maybe a mile or so on simplex.

The "magnetic-mount" antenna is actually a very versatile option, depending on the actual antenna used. Some are available using rare-earth magnets with a short whip (12"-18") and are very usable on VHF and UHF. Other mounts are available that will accept any antenna designed for that mount. We have a Larsen VHF/UHF antenna on a magnetic mount on our Jeep at this time. It was permanently mounted on our last pickup truck, and will be again soon on the Patriot, but for the moment it is a magnetic-mount.

The magnetic mount also works well when traveling in another person's vehicle, with either a mobile on a lighter plug (must use low power to prevent blowing the lighter plug fuses), or a handie-talkie with a connector adaptor between the radio and antenna. Some of these with shorter whips and about 12 feet of coax will fit into a backpack or bag.

The "Roll-Up J-Pole" is an antenna made from approximately 60 inches of flat TV twin-lead and a short run of coax. This is an easy DIY project, or it may be purchased commercially. As the name implies, it easily rolls up to fit into a backpack or bag. When needed, the antenna is unrolled, pulled up into a tree with string or rope, placed on a pole, or tacked to a wall and connected to the handheld or mobile radio.

The antenna we use on our handheld radios is the Nagoya® NA-771 15.6" whip antenna. These antennas WORK! I have been able to use repeaters 5-6 miles away from inside the house, and 15 or more miles away when standing outside.

Noting the test results that were reported by substituting the antenna which came with the handheld radio with a Nagoya® 701 antenna, this seems like a 'must do' item for everyone and all situations. The Nagoya® 701 antenna is about the same weight and 3″ longer (7¾") but still more than sufficiently portable for almost all situations.

Be careful, though, as there are some knock-offs out there for under $10 which will not give the same performance as the "Authentic Genuine Nagoya® NA-771". Expect to pay around $17-$20 at the time of this writing, in 2019, and be sure to order the right connection for your selected radios. You won't regret the investment.

Mistakes In Prepper Communications

Buying unnecessary equipment or gadgets

There are a lot of 'gadgets' offered to radio operators. Some are useful, most are not. Be sure that accessories you purchase solve a problem you have and don't create a problem you don't have.

External microphones have a purpose with handheld radios, especially when attaching an earphone for private listening, or in noisy environments when the radio is worn on the belt and the microphone is clipped to clothing near the ear, but aren't needed for most applications.

Not understanding equipment limitations

There are limitations to every piece of equipment available. Too many people buy a small handheld radio and expect it to do everything with it, and are disappointed that it does not meet their expectations. I was one of them.

We cover antennas in more detail in another place, but the antenna that comes with most handheld radios is not sufficient for most applications covering any distance at all. It is unreasonable to expect a "rubber duck" antenna to cover the distance required to make contact in all but the most limited circumstances. The 'cap antenna" that attaches to the user's ball cap experiences the same issues. They aren't a bad idea for certain applications, such as using at hamfests, festivals, and where range is limited to a few hundred yards at most.

There is a vast difference in theoretical transmitting distances and practical transmitting distances. Don't expect the twenty-six mile blister pack radios to work across an actual twenty six miles. In our experience, the best we have obtained is about four miles under ideal conditions.

Not having a communications plan

You have the radio; you have the license; disaster hits. Who are you going to talk to? Do you know which repeaters are in your local area? Do you know which ones can operate on emergency power? Do you know which repeater is used by the local ARES (amateur radio emergency services) group? Have you programmed those repeaters in? Have you practiced using them?

Most of the ham radio units popular in the prepping community are not very intuitive to program manually, and require some practice to operate proficiently.

Our radios are programmed, we have a list of them handy, and family members have the same on their end. We have a plan on which repeaters to use to pass messages back and forth and we have a plan for using internet-based repeaters for contacting each other in an emergency. We can also use HF frequencies to talk across great distances if needed. Each family member knows that it may take a day or two to get the messages through, but we know where to be 'looking' for each other.

Chapter 8

Every Day Carry

Let's talk about the things that we should carry with us every day. We'll divide those into four categories or ways to carry: On-body, EDC bag, Go bag, and GOOD (get out of Dodge) bag. Included are items you may use regularly and some you need rarely, but definitely want, "just in case".

On-Body

Our "on-body" items are obviously those things we carry in our pockets, on our belt, or wear directly on the body, such as a watch, paracord bracelet, knife, multi-tool, flashlight, or firearm.

Your individual on-body items will vary, but should include wallet with cash, identification, and a printed list of emergency contact information. You'll certainly want to carry your cell phone, small flashlight, and a pocket-sized folding knife and/or a multi-tool (or both). Depending on your local and state laws, and your employer's policies, you may wish to carry a handgun on your body for self-protection.

Paul Markel (www.studentofthegun.com) says that EDC should include something sharp (knife), something bright (flashlight), something medical (IFAK, tourniquet, or bandages), and something lethal (handgun).

EDC Bag

Paul Markel (www.studentofthegun.com) says that EDC (Every Day Carry) should include something sharp (knife), something bright (flashlight), something medical (IFAK, tourniquet, or bandages), and something lethal (handgun).

Our "EDC bag" is for items that are larger or too cumbersome to carry on body, are needed less often, but still needed regularly, and ones you don't want to be without: medications, insect repellent, fire starter, first-aid kit or "boo boo" kit, phone chargers, and smaller 'kits' such as an Altoids tin emergency kit with safety pins, tape, sewing needle for emergency repairs, even a few breath mints. This is the place to carry those little items you need once in a while.

You might also consider carrying a pen and notebook, a handkerchief or bandana, Bic lighter, a second knife, a second flashlight and extra batteries, multi-tool, tourniquet, small tool kit, snacks and a bottle of water. For those who carry firearms, extra magazines of ammo can go in the EDC bag as well.

Mark: *"Recently we were in a friend's cabin in the mountains near Blue Ridge, Georgia. the first night, I had a king-sized case of indigestion. (It wasn't Krista's cooking, as we ate out on our way in.) We had forgotten to pack our OTC meds for indigestion. Krista had some Alka-Seltzer in her bag that got me through the night. The next morning, I checked the med kit in my EDC bag and there was my stash of a half dozen Omeprazole capsules. Problem solved.*

Speaking of our med-kit, that is simply a Ziploc bag of various medications that may be needed from time to time, such as pain reliever, allergy pills, anti-diarrhea tablets, and a few days' supply of our regular medications.

Kits can be made for any number of situations. One we carry is a cell charger cable kit. It has wall charger, lighter plug charger, USB cable, and an extension cable.

We also have a couple of extra AA batteries and a pair of CR-123 batteries, spares for our flashlights, in a small Ziploc bag.

Select a bag that blends well with your personal situation. A messenger bag or leather brief case WILL blend better than a camouflage tactical backpack with MOLLE pouches. A laptop bag works well in an office environment, whether or not you carry a laptop. The laptop backpack style works very well, and isn't questioned when carried into most any environment.

We both carry a cross-body bag that is about 8"x12"x4" and has several pockets. Krista calls hers a purse. Mark calls his a 'possibles bag.' Both carry many of the items above, plus extra reading glasses, hand sanitizer, pocket-sized packet of wet wipes, and personal items to meet our individual needs. This bag goes everywhere, and rarely stays in the car.

Go Bag

The items in our "Go bag" are the things we seldom need, but are invaluable in an emergency. These are the items that will help us get home after a disaster or survive being stranded for hours or even days on the highway or in a snow storm.

This is the 'go everywhere bag', and stays in the car. Some people call it a "get home bag." We have never had to use it to get home, but we have used it for many other reasons. This is the bag in which you carry those things you really hope you don't have to use as well as many things you know you will at some time, and will really be glad you had it when you needed it. It carries the things that you would need IF you did have to try to get home on foot, in any number of situations.

You certainly don't have to carry them all, and your list will vary, but here's a list of things you might consider carrying in your Go bag:

Water filter, such as a Sawyer mini

Two or more bottles of water (can be attached to water filter)

Single-walled metal water bottle & water (can be used for heating water)

Quality fixed-blade knife & sheath

Multi-tool

Small tool kit

A change of clothes, socks, and old walking shoes

First-aid kit (larger than the EDC first-aid kit, extra tourniquet, bandages)

Sunscreen

Insect repellent

Fire starting kit, including dry tinder

Fishing kit (25-30' of line, hooks, and sinkers, in a very small snap-top container)

Extra flashlight or headband light

Extra batteries

Rain poncho (if you pay $2 for it, it's a bread wrapper, not a poncho)

Space blankets or emergency blankets

Cordage, such as twine and paracord

Hygiene kit (including toilet paper)

Feminine hygiene kit for the ladies

Compass

Signaling mirror

Whistle

Two-way radio

Extra ammo for your EDC gun

A .22 caliber handgun & ammo (suitable for small game) if legal, and you're plan for this bag is getting home on foot over several days.

No-cook food items: jerky, nuts, dried fruit, peanut butter, etc,

EZ-prep food items, powdered soup packets, ramen noodles, pop-top canned items which can be heated in the can, chunky soups and stews, chili, etc. which can be heated on a small fire or eaten cold if necessary.

In the event you are faced with a "get-home" situation requiring you to leave your vehicle and hoof it to safety, combine all the kits you have, taking what you can carry, prioritizing the items, and leaving the rest behind. Be prepared to survive as you go, whether it is in the woods building a shelter for the night, sleeping under a bridge, or staying the night in any safe shelter you can find.

GOOD bag (Get Out Of Dodge)

The "GOOD bag" allows you to leave your home at a moments' notice, without taking the time to pack. It contains the things you wouldn't normally carry around with you. This bag would have several changes of clothes, sturdy shoes, and anything else you would need (but not have in your EDC bag or car bag) to make it several days. This would be that bag you would grab, along with the other two, in the event of a sudden evacuation. You might wish to have thumb drives, flash drives, or external hard drives backing up your computer, as well as scans of all your important documents, just in case your house was destroyed by fire or flood.

This isn't so much a survival bag as it is a bag that allows you to leave the house very quickly when the need arises. It could be a fast-approaching wild fire, a house fire next door threatening your house, the need to go to a storm shelter, or a family emergency requiring you to hurry to another location, such as a hospital or other family member's home.

This bag should contain a couple of complete changes of clothes, including underwear and socks. Add in enough no-prep-required foods and snacks to make it a couple of days. It helps to not have to eat out of hospital vending machines.

There are times it may become necessary to quickly Get Out Of Dodge. Your GOOD bag saves precious time.

Chapter 9

Spiritual Preparedness

If you are offended by God, The Bible, or spiritual things, just skip this chapter.

It may have been Zig Ziglar that said, "We'll be dead a lot longer than we will be alive, so we had better make preparations for after we die."

Hebrews 9:27 says, "It is appointed unto man once to die, and after that, the judgment." The words "after that" indicate that there is something to come after we die.

As Christians, we believe the Bible is the infallible Word of God, it is true, and is does not change. In other words, the Bible is as relevant today as it was the day His words were recorded.

The Bible says that there are two possible places of residence after we die, Heaven, in the presence of God, and Hell, a place of eternal torment in the absence of God.

The Apostle Paul says in Philippians 1:21 that for the Christian "death is gain." To be absent from the body (dead) is to be in the presence of God. Scripture makes it plain that the true Christian resides in Heaven after death. It makes clear that salvation from our sin is not something we earn. It's not something we can work for. It is not a balance scale where our good and our bad are weighed out and if we do more good that bad, we can be accepted into Heaven after we die.

The standard to qualify on our own, is being sinless, but Romans 3:10- "There is none righteous, not one"- means that not one of us is without sin. Not one of us deserves to go to Heaven. However, Jesus Christ made a way for us through His death on the cross of Calvary. He, being sinless, took our place and paid the price for sin, and offers salvation to us. It is a free gift to us, but cost Him dearly.

Jesus is the only Son of God, completely man and completely God, and through His death on the cross, forgiveness for our sin was offered. In Ephesians 7:8, the Lord inspired Paul to write, "By grace, we are saved through faith, not of our own doing - it is the gift of God." To be saved is to know that you are a sinner, that you believe Jesus died on the cross to pay that sin-debt, to believe He rose from death fully alive, that He went to be with His Father in Heaven, and that you trust Him to be your personal Savior, the Lord of your life. If you prayed words to this effect, sincerely from your heart, then the Holy Spirit will dwell with you, in your heart and life, and you are indeed saved. If you're already a believer, we rejoice with you as fellow believers!

Spiritual "prepping" to us means reading, studying, and learning the Scripture (we suggest starting with the New Testament Gospel of John for new believers) and spending time in devotional prayer in a quiet place regularly. God is alive and well, and wants to grow you and bless you as you walk down your individual road of life. Ask God to help you understand the Bible as you read it with new spiritual perspective, and pray for His divine wisdom for life here on earth in the decisions you make and in the ways you choose to live for His glory and honor. Spiritual prepping also means associating with other believers in a church or group that honors God's Word and lives by it. Preppers often share their earthly goods with others, and spiritual preppers do the same with their faith - tell others of your faith in Christ, and of the things He has done in your life. You won't be perfect, you will stumble on your journey, now and then, we all do. Our salvation doesn't "come and go" when we sin - if it did, then His death on the cross would never be enough to save us, would it?

Times of crisis or disaster often drive people to evaluate "the big picture", especially when they've escaped death. Their thoughts and behaviors take on a whole new set of priorities, as material things fade from importance. Questions of purpose and destiny often arise, and many find themselves woefully wanting in the area of faith. Prepping one's pantry is important, but it is our prayer and hope that you will take stock in your spiritual preparedness for eternal security and peace.

Scripture says that He took our place in death, and arose on the third day, having conquered death and the penalty for sin. Over five hundred people saw him after his resurrection and his ascension into Heaven was witnessed by many. Today, He sits at the right hand of God, awaiting the day He returns to take His children home. We believe that is an actual day in history when He will do as God's Word says. We do not know when that will be, as the Bible says that no man knows, except the Father (God).

The Scripture states clearly that there is only one way to Heaven and that Way is through Jesus Christ.

Acts 4:12 says "There is no other name given among men whereby you must be saved."

Scripture is also clear what happens to the ones who die without having accepted the free gift of salvation offered by Jesus Christ. Revelation 20:11-15, the passage known as the 'Great White Throne Judgment' reveals the judgment of the lost, people who rejected Jesus Christ. God's words will be, "Depart from Me, I never knew you."

What a sad time it will be for multitudes who will realize that their choice in rejecting Jesus Christ as their personal Savior has resulted in their spending eternity in Hell.

Eternity - that is time without end. Forever.

The choice is yours.

Chapter 10

Knives and Bladed Tools

A quality fixed-blade knife is one of the most versatile pieces of equipment the prepper can possess. Many things can be accomplished in the wilderness with nothing but a survival knife. If there is a single "must have" piece of equipment, it would be a quality knife.

The survival knife must be strong and of good quality. Here are some qualities of a good survival knife:

Full tang – the tang of a knife is the portion of the blade that extends down into the handles or "scales". The handles of a full tang knife are attached to the tang, giving the knife strength. The tangs of cheaper knives that re usually inserted into the handle and may break off with heavy duty use. Hollow handled knives (made for storing things in the handle) may sound nice, but decrease the knife's strength.

There is great debate on which is the better material for a knife -- carbon steel or stainless steel. Stainless steel can last a long time without rusting, but may not hold an edge as long as carbon steel. Carbon steel is easier to sharpen to a fine edge, but will rust faster than stainless steel. It is personal preference. Both are good.

Blade length is also important. Too short, and it doesn't do the job needed; too long, and it becomes hard to use (for some jobs) and much harder to carry. Most survival knives are in the range of six to twelve inches. Choose one that is comfortable in your hand and is well-balanced.

The blade design is critical in choosing a survival knife. A straight blade will work much better when chopping wood. A straight blade can be sharpened in the field with a smooth stone, where a serrated blade usually takes a special sharpener and a very specialized skill to do by hand.

A blade thickness of three-sixteenth inch to one-quarter inch will make an extremely solid knife, able to stand up to chopping and batoning. Batoning is using the knife to split wood while striking the spine of the knife with a stick or mallet to drive it through the wood. Though not ideal, and hard on the knife, this thickness blade could be used for digging as well.

Sheaths are the often overlooked part of a knife system, and come in about as many varieties as there are knives, and it is a personal choice. Some attach to the belt, some have a tie-down to keep it from flopping around while walking, some strap around the thigh or calf, and others attach to the straps of a backpack. The purpose of the sheath is to keep the knife safe and secure. Choose one that fits the knife and has a secure strap to hold it in place, and fits your preferred carry method.

Avoid gimmicky knives. We loved these as youngsters. You might have a compass in the handle, or could unscrew the cap where you had stored matches, fishing line, fire starter, or any number of "survival items." Not really a bad idea, but the structural security of the knife is diminished, or it is made of poor quality material, or items like the compass will make it harder to grip, especially if wet.

In the era of our growing up, a young man absolutely had to have a pocketknife. It was a right of passage from a child to a young man, and often gifted by a parent or grandparent. That knife went everywhere, marbles in one pocket and a pocketknife in the other, even to school (times have changed).

As we got older, we carried a slightly higher-quality pocketknife. Some of us chose a very high quality pocketknife, but others still have that early version. Though no longer carried, it still holds a place of honor and brings back many memories.

Knife Sharpening

There are four basic types of knife sharpeners: electrical, manual, honing steel and stone. Each has its place, with pros and cons.

The electrical sharpener is often used in kitchens by many amateur and professional chefs, or installed on a workbench. It is quick to put an edge on a knife, but is not portable, and requires electricity.

The manual sharpener is a handheld device that is pulled along the length of the blade edge. Often containing ceramic rods set at the proper angle, both sides of the blade are sharpened at once.

Sharpening steels, or honing rods, are usually a tapered piece of steel with very fine ridges along its length, with a wooden or plastic handle. The steel rod is a very fast way to touch up the edge on a knife.

A sharpening stone, or whetstone, is the most popular way to sharpen anything from a pocketknife to a large survival knife.

Machete, Hatchet, or Axe

An axe is an awesome tool to have at home or in an off-road vehicle, but rather cumbersome to carry around. That is where a machete or hatchet shines--portability.

A sturdy machete will prove invaluable for building shelter, cutting through brush, or chopping firewood. Slightly more cumbersome than a hatchet, a machete can be carried in, or strapped to, a backpack.

There are a number of lightweight hatchets available, suitable for camping, hiking, and carrying "just in case." Some hatchets come with a belt sheath, and others can be carried in a backpack or strapped onto the pack. The hatchet is a better tool than a machete for splitting wood.

Arkansas Stones

The Arkansas sharpening stone is the most popular of all the stones for hand-sharpening, and are of very high quality. They are available in varying degrees of grit, or coarseness, from approximately 600 grit to over 2500 grit.

The "Coarse Arkansas" stone is the coarsest stone and is usually gray or off-white. The coarse stone is for very dull blades that need to have a proper bevel angle put on them. It quickly cuts away material, saving time over using the finer stones.

The "Fine Arkansas" is the next stone in the lineup; it begins to refine the edge on the blade.

The "Soft Arkansas" stone puts a sharp edge on the blade while leaving a little "tooth" to the edge, and is usually off-white or marbled with gray or orange.

The "Hard Arkansas" stone will put a fine edge on your blade, even to the point of shaving. Using it produces a fine edge that appears more polished.

The "Hard Black Arkansas" or black surgical stone, needs a very sharp edge to begin, but will take the edge to razor sharp and a mirror finish. These stones were used to sharpen surgical scalpels when they were reused and sharpened by hand.

The "Hard Translucent" stone is much like the Hard Black Arkansas, and both leave a polished, almost mirrored, razor-sharp finish. The color varies slightly from stone to stone, but if held up to light it is translucent.

Diamond Stones

Diamond stones are flat surfaces covered with micro diamonds or diamond dust. The diamond stones, like Arkansas stones, are used for hand-sharpening and come in different grits or coarseness: extra-coarse, coarse, fine, and extra fine.

Diamond stones, though not quite as popular, do put a great edge on a knife.

Ceramic Stones

Ceramic stones will put a keen edge on a blade, and are available in flat or round. The round stones, or rods, are often found in systems when put together produce a

"V" shape. The blade is drawn down the rod and alternated between sides of the blade. Ceramics are harder than oil stones and will cut through almost any alloy or exotic steel, saving time and effort.

The bottom line on sharpening is to have a way to sharpen your blades, whether it is a pocketknife, survival knife, machete, axe, or hatchet. An electric system for the shop or garage (I have one) is fine, but have a system that is portable and does not require electricity.

Caring for your knife

All knives must be cared for, regardless of the type of steel used in the making.

Stainless steel would be more properly called corrosion-resistant steel, as it will rust if not cared for. Stainless steel is also harder to sharpen. Steels, like 440 carbon and above, create an edge that is easier to sharpen and holds an edge longer, but requires more care. If you are in inclement weather, or regularly around salt water, stainless steel may be the only reasonable choice for your knife.

First off, your knife must be kept sharp. Some have said a dull knife is useless and dangerous. Get a good set of honing stones and learn to put a keen edge on your blade.

Keep a check on your blade for small rust spots. These can be polished away with a bit of fine steel wool or polishing paste. Your knife needs to have a fine coat of oil on the blade. Don't overdo it; a thin coat will delay rusting. If you are using the knife as a skinning knife, use a food-grade mineral oil to keep from tainting the meat.

Leather sheaths need to be cleaned with saddle soap from time to time, and mink oil applied about once per year to keep the leather from cracking or becoming brittle.

Store your knives in their sheath, in a dry place, and, with regular care, they should last for several lifetimes, and can be passed down to children and grandchildren to become a cherished item. Be sure to tell them stories and experiences associated with the knife. It will make owning it all the more special.

Knife safety

There are a million ways to hurt yourself in the wild, or around the house; careless handling of razor-sharp bladed tools WILL make that *easier*. Here's a few basic safety rules for the proper handling and care of knives and blades:

- Cut away from you – if you slip, you don't want to stab yourself.

- Keep a firm grip – liquids and blood make the handle very slippery.

- Keep eyes on what you are doing – now is not the time to multi-task.

- Take your time; there is usually no need to get in a hurry, which can cause accidents.

- Don't grab or kick at a falling knife - like buttered bread hitting the floor butter side down, the odds of grabbing the knife by the blade is great. Just let it hit the ground, then pick it up, and go back at it.

- When handing a knife to someone else, offer it handle first, or lay it down and let them pick it up.

- When walking, put the knife in its sheath (safest) or carry it point down, edge to the back, and toss it away from you if you fall.

- Keep your off-hand fingers away from the cutting instrument.

- Use 2 hands to close a folding knife - sure, we've all done it, but it can bite you.

- Keep it sharp. Some say a dull knife is more dangerous, and a sharp blade is certainly easier to use.

Chapter 11

Small Kits You Can Build

It can be handy to have several small kits made to be put into your bag for day trips, traveling, or special needs. We have made these kits in empty Altoid tins, but small snap-top containers, smokeless tobacco cans, medicine bottles, even Ziploc bags can be used.

Fishing Kit

For those who want to prepare for longer-term survival situations away from home, a fishing kit is a handy option to have. The kit can be small yet still contain enough to catch fish when needed. An old Altoids tin, small plastic container, even an old smokeless tobacco container can be used. Twenty to thirty feet of six- to ten-pound-test fishing line, some lead sinkers in various sizes, and a half-dozen or more various sized hooks should suffice. Grubs and insects can be found under logs, leaves, and around plants, and you could dig for worms.

In an area with bamboo growing, you can cut one for a ready-made fishing pole. A long green limb can be cut from a tree for a pole, or a six- to eight-inch piece of a stick can be used to anchor the line for a hand-line. The line can be tied to a branch over or near the water and the bait left for a period of time, checked replenished as necessary. The branch gives the line some flexibility to keep it from being broken as a fish pulls against it.

A *Fishing Kit* should contain 25-35 feet of fishing line, several hooks of different sizes, and a few lead weights. Depending on your location, a few fly-fishing flies might be of use. Tightly wrap the fishing line around a small wooden dowel or section of a pencil and hold it in place with a piece of tape. Six- to ten-pound-test line works well, but use what you have.

Use tape to hold the hooks together so they don't tangle with other items in the kit. The lead sinkers can go in loose, or be affixed to tape like the hooks. Depending on the size of the container, small bobbers can be added as well as flies.

Hand lines can be made when needing to fish, or a pole may be made from a flexible limb or branch. Worms, grasshoppers, moths, or other bait can be found near the water. It won't be like fishing with a nice rod and reel, or even an old-fashioned cane pole, but it could put food in your tummy if you are lost in the woods for an extended period of time.

"Boo Boo" Kit

An Emergency Kit or *"boo boo"* kit, is a great little kit for all kinds of daily "emergencies", like a broken zipper, a cut finger, a lost button, a splinter, or any number of those little things we experience along life's way.

This kit includes items such as a small BIC lighter, safety pins, straight pins, band-aids, a sewing needle and thread, an eyeglass repair kit, tweezers, or anything else you think you might need. Our kits are in old Altoid tins, and carry well in a purse or small EDC bag.

One man made a number of different kits, all in smokeless tobacco cans. He put six of the cans together and covered them with shrink-wrap, making a roll. He carries the roll in his glove box. When he needs to be away from his truck, he throws it in his bag or backpack. It gives him a pretty good survival kit which could solve quite a few problems if he had to hoof it back home or spend the night in the woods.

Individual First-Aid Kit   (IFAK)

Individual first-aid kits can be as simple or as complex as you wish to make them, but should be able to handle the simple to the complex.

A daily pocket-sized kit could be carried to cover minor injuries with items such as band-aids, alcohol preps, and maybe an antibiotic cream packet.

The EDC bag could contain a slightly larger kit, including all of the above plus sting kill, burn cream, and assorted over-the-counter medications, small bandage, a roll of gauze, and a tourniquet.

The Go Bag could contain even more first-aid supplies including dressings of various sizes (4x4, 6x9 etc), SAM splint, Quick-Clot, chest seal, elastic wrap, cold pack, waterproof medical tape, etc. This would be the kit to use if you happen up on an automobile accident or hunting accident. When assembling your bag, you're limited only by its size, your funds, your training, and your imagination.

Mark: *"I had a small hand wound recently and needed a band-aid. I told someone riding with me that there were at least three first-aid kits in the vehicle. With those I could handle a gunshot wound, knife wound, sucking chest wound, even a limb amputation but I didn't have a single band-aid at the time. I had fallen into the trap of preparing for the major injuries (which most of us rarely encounter) and failed to prepare for a simple, everyday run-of-the-mill "emergency."*

Here are some first-aid items you might wish to consider carrying:

Latex or Nitrile gloves

Band-aids (cures all kinds of boo-boos)

Bandages of various sizes (2x2, 4x4, 5x7, 6x9)

Rolled gauze

Medical tape

Safety pins

Tweezers

Scissors

EMT shears (cuts almost anything)

Tourniquet

Quickclot, clotting spray, or hemostatic guaze

Bandana or triangular bandage

OTC medications, including aspirin for chest pain

Hydrocortisone cream

Sunscreen

Antiseptic cream

Alcohol preps

Alcohol-free wipes

Eye drops

Hand sanitizer

Cold and heat packs

Flashlight (AA battery)

Emergency blanket

Dermabond, liquid bandage, or super glue

Chest seal

Butterfly bandages

Steri-strips

CPR mask

Finger splints

SAM splint-a lightweight, moldable splint

If possible, maintain a minimum thirty-day supply of
all prescription medications, especially life-sustaining
medications, including insulin, respiratory inhalers,
nitroglycerine, and epinephrine pens.

Fire-Starting Kit

The practical prepper will have multiple methods of starting fire, but the objective is getting a fire going fast. Knowing how to start a fire with a bow drill is a good skill to have, but bow drills are difficult, take time, practice, and are not the most efficient.

The good ol' Bic lighter is much faster and easier when it comes to getting a fire started. Get three, and buy the Bic brand. The cheaper off-brands, which come from the dollar stores, tend to be less dependable and less sturdy.

Storm matches, water-proof matches, and wax covered matches work well also, especially in wet weather.

Steel wool and a nine-volt battery will work by placing the steel wool across both the positive and negative posts of the battery. Be careful, it can get very hot and very quickly, but is an effective option for starting fire.

A ferrocerium rod, or ferro rod, is a man-made metallic alloy substance that, when scraped with a rough or sharp edge, like the back of a knife blade or a piece of a saw blade, will produce sparks in excess of five-thousand degrees.

Tinder is needed to start your fire. Fine little pieces of wood, cloth, and even corn chips will work. We keep a large medicine bottle filled with fatwood in each of our bags. It can be shaved to small slivers and using a ferro rod, flint and steel, or a mechanical fire starter, a fire can be made. The quarter-inch diameter cut to four inches long works well with a Bic lighter or matches.

Cotton balls permeated with petroleum jelly make great tinder, as does dryer lint and petroleum jelly stuffed inside a toilet paper tube. Peel back a little of the tube to form a place for sparks to land if using a ferro rod or flint and steel; if using a lighter or matches just light the end of the tube.

Magnesium is a good fire starter, but must be cut or scraped to build a little pile of shavings to receive a spark. One trick is to pre-shave magnesium and store it in a medicine bottle for use when needed. If you have the fire starter-rod that is connected to the magnesium bar, you may find it best to store it in a small Ziploc bag, otherwise it will get on everything in your bag.

Commercial tinder is available under several names. It's easy to pack and easy to use. Two of our favorites are Tinder Quik (waterproof) and Wet Fire, which burns wet or dry. That comes in handy when trying to start a fire in wet weather.

We recommend a sturdy knife for shaving tinder or to baton wood, and a machete or hatchet for chopping wood.

Tinder Kit

A Tinder Kit keeps dry tender available for use when needed. Ours contain a small supply of fatwood, some cotton balls, and petroleum jelly. You could make a very small container of shaved magnesium or magnesium powder to save a lot of time when you need it.

Lights-out Kit

A "lights-out kit" can be contained in something as simple as an old shoebox, easily accessible in the dark (though a good prepper will likely have a small flashlight on their person on within easy reach at all times). Larger items will require larger containers, or may be stored separately. Items could include:

Flashlights

Extra batteries for every device

Headlamps or cap lights

Candles, matches, and lighters

Small LED lanterns

Propane lantern for larger areas

Rechargeable batteries and solar charger for longer events

We have included a power inverter to use with the battery from our car to run our wireless network, computer, TV for local news, ham radio, and Mark's CPAP machine (vital for Krista's sleep).

Chapter 12

Firearms

We believe in personal responsibility. This is the major reason we are practical preppers. We take responsibility for our own safety and provisions the best we are able.

We also take responsibility for our own personal protection in that we both legally carry concealed weapons. It is true that, "When seconds count, police are minutes away."

Carrying a firearm is a personal decision, and requires some decisions be made beforehand, such as to get some **good** training with your firearm. Practice is not training. Find a good instructor and invest in a few hours of personal training, or take a firearms class. A CCW class is not enough. It simply fulfills the legal requirement for some states. If you have decades of experience with a firearm, keep training.

What is the purpose of the firearm? Is it for sporting purposes only, such as target shooting or hunting? That's fine, buy a quality firearm you will enjoy, keep it unloaded and locked away until you take it to the range or field.

Is it for personal defense? Before buying or carrying a firearm for defense, you must answer the question, "Can I pull the trigger in defense of myself or another person?" Many initially say, "No," but when questioned further, they come to the conclusion that they *could* pull the trigger to save the lives of their children, grand children, or aged parents. It is a personal decision that *must* be made before buying or carrying a firearm for personal defense.

One lady was talking with me and said that there was no way she could shoot someone else. I asked if she had children. She said that she had three, two daughters and a son. I asked to what length she would go to protect those children is someone was trying to hurt those children or sexually assault one of her two daughters. I saw her some weeks later and she said that she had been thinking and had come to the decision that she could, in fact, shoot someone to protect her family. She is now seeking firearm training and purchasing a handgun for personal and family protection.

With that said, let's consider some firearms useful in various situations, as well as some of the pros and cons of each.

Home Defense

There is a huge debate in the firearm/prepper world as to what is the "best" firearm for home defense. It comes down to two basic choices: the pump shotgun, or the semi-automatic rifle. We won't settle that argument here (or anywhere else) but either can be great choices for home defense.

Long Guns

Rifles and shotguns have the advantage over handguns in power and in accuracy, and in some cases, ammo capacity: power, because of larger and faster, (or both) bullets and more powder; accuracy, because of a longer distance between the front and rear sights, and longer barrels.

The rifle has the advantage over the shotgun when it comes to effective distance. The rifle is the only firearm with an effective range of a thousand yards or more, in the appropriate hands, and one hundred to two hundred yards in the hands of the average shooter.

The shotgun has the advantage in versatility. Though limited to fifty to one hundred yards, depending on whether buckshot or slugs are loaded, the shotgun can be used to hunt deer, caribou, and elk, or to defend yourself from wolves or bears.

The shotgun, depending on the size of the shot, can be used to hunt small game and waterfowl, as well as inland birds, such as turkey, doves, quail, and pheasants.

The shotgun is also an excellent choice for home defense.

The Pump Shotgun

Many have said that the mere sound of "racking" (chambering) a pump shotgun is enough to send even the most nefarious running. Some believe all you have to do is point it in the general direction and pull the trigger to hit the target.

Neither could be further from the truth. The sound of a pump shotgun being racked is a distinctive, unmistakable sound, and will send the prudent on his way, but those who are willing to take the risks involved in a home invasion may be headstrong, unafraid of being injured or killed. Being hyped up on drugs often exacerbates the situation.

Buckshot fired out of an eighteen-inch barreled shotgun will spread at a rate of approximately one inch per yard traveled. Therefore, at a distance of fifteen feet the pattern is approximately five inches wide. You must aim the shotgun to be effective in a defensive situation.

Rifles

The Semi-Automatic Rifle

A semi-automatic sporting rifle is far superior to a bolt-action rifle for home defense, simply because of the rate of fire and the ammo capacity of each. Reloading is quicker in the case of magazine-fed rifles.

At this time, the AR-15 in .223 caliber is the most popular sporting rifle in America, and is a great choice for home defense. With proper ammo choices, the .223 can be used for hunting animals up to and including white tailed deer. For predator animal control, like feral hogs or coyotes, it's almost perfect.

Semi-auto Survival Rifles

The "survival rifle" goes back to a weapon designed for U.S. Air Force survival kits. Several are available today as a .22LR, nine-shot, semi-automatic rifle that breaks down and stores in the floating stock to make for a rifle suitable to be carried in a boat, canoe, vehicle, or backpack. It could be used to provide food along the way if you are forced to make a multi-day trek home or if lost in the woods.

Bolt-Action Rifles

Accuracy...........

The bolt-action rifle, especially when equipped with a scope, is generally accepted as the most accurate rifle, and is an excellent choice for hunting. Available in a multitude of calibers, the bolt-action is suitable for vermin and every type of game, from small to the large.

The .243, .270. and .30-06 are the most popular calibers for North American deer hunting. They are very accurate and very easy to operate.

A .22 LR bolt action makes an excellent youth rifle when learning to handle a firearm, as well as being a good firearm for putting food on the table.

Pros and Cons of Rifles and Shotguns

The pump shotgun comes with fairly substantial recoil, especially in 12 gauge. The 20 gauge shotgun has less recoil, though still noticeable, and may be easier to control by younger shooters and those averse to recoil.

Most pump shotguns will hold five to eight rounds, and can be plugged to hold only three rounds, which means they can legally be used for bird hunting.

The pump shotgun is very versatile. There are shells are available for bird hunting (#7 or #8 shot), turkey hunting (#4 shot), rabbit and squirrel hunting (#6 shot), as well as deer hunting (00 buckshot and slugs).

Shotguns are effective at much closer distances than most rifles, but are effective out to around fifty yards with buckshot and a maximum of around one hundred yards with slugs, in most cases.

The pump shotgun is readily available at most sporting goods stores that sell firearms, and are reasonably inexpensive.

The .223 AR-15 has almost no recoil. It can easily be handled by almost anyone, including young children (with adult supervision). They are also a "ton of fun."

Lighter than most pump shotguns, the AR-15 can be carried longer and over greater distances.

There are a variety of bullets available for the .223, and several companies recognize that there is a market for good hunting rounds. It's a great rifle for youth and those sensitive to recoil.

The AR-15 is available in a wide range of price levels; $500 being an average entry-level rifle up to several thousand dollars for a customized top-tier rifle. It's available in a range of calibers, from .22 long rifle to 300 Black Out, and even .308 (AR-10), which will take down any animal native to North America.

Handguns

The major advantage a handgun has over a rifle or shotgun is concealability, as well as the ability to be carried "hands free," and in very close quarters, maneuverability. A good holster makes a handgun available at all times, while allowing both hands to be available for other tasks.

There are two basic categories we will discuss here; revolvers and pistols (semi-automatics). There are advantages and disadvantages to each.

Revolvers

The revolver has the advantage in simplicity and reliability.

Revolver capacity is five, six, or seven rounds, and in the case of the .22LR, nine rounds. The revolver requires less training to learn to use than does a semi-automatic. Therefore, in the hands of the "untrained" or the shooter with minimal training, the revolver has a slight advantage in safety and usability. Most revolvers do not have external safeties that must be manipulated to make the firearm able to fire and manipulated again to make the firearm safe. The trigger simply needs to be pulled for the firearm to function, and is completely safe as long as the trigger is not pulled.

The revolver has the advantage in dependability, as they are much less likely to experience a malfunction, and if a round fails to fire, pulling the trigger again advances the cylinder to the next round. There are no failures to feed, no double feeds, and no "stove-pipe" jams that must be cleared.

Some five shot revolvers are small enough to be comfortably carried in a pocket (not without a pocket holster), light enough to be carried all day, and available in enough calibers to cover most any need from personal protection, (whether it be from two- or four-legged predators), to putting meat on the table.

Revolvers enjoy some advantage in power, and are available in the very powerful .500 S&W Magnum, .45-70, .45 Long Colt, and .44 Magnum. Granted, there are a few .50 and .44 magnum caliber semi-autos available, but generally speaking, the larger, more powerful calibers are more often available in revolvers.

Semi-Auto (pistol)

Semi-automatic pistols have a longer learning curve to proficiency than a revolver, in the hands of the less well-trained.

The semi-auto pistol has the advantage in capacity and reloading speed. Many compacts have a capacity of ten or more rounds, and full-sized pistols can hold fifteen to nineteen rounds. Most semi-autos are magazine (not clip) fed. The magazine holds a single or double stack of ammo, and is inserted into the handle of the pistol. After each round is fired, the blowback of the rounds fired causes the slide to move to the rear, ejecting the spent cartridge as it does. A spring causes the slide to again move forward, causing another round to be stripped from the magazine and loaded into the firing chamber. It does all this automatically. "Semi" is used to indicate that the trigger must be pulled each time a round is fired. (Full-auto indicates that rounds are fired until the trigger is released or the ammo runs out). Reloading is faster since the empty magazine is ejected, a fresh one is inserted, and a new round can be loaded into the firing chamber.

No one gun will do all things well. No one firearm is suitable for every purpose. A .22 Long Rifle will make a bear angry. Using a bear gun to introduce your girlfriend to shooting (thought funny by some idiots) WILL create an angry girlfriend! It will also turn her away from firearms, and is a childish thing to do.

Putting Food On The Table

Some of us grew up hunting, and many hunt today to put meat on the table. Some hunt for the enjoyment of the woods and rarely harvest an animal unless they already know who would like to have the meat. No one who respects the outdoors and wildlife will be guilty of wasting our natural resources by needlessly killing animals for the sake of killing. We eat what we kill or we give the meat to someone who will.

Small Game

Small game, such as rabbits and squirrels, can be hunted with .22 caliber rifles, and even .22 caliber pistols, as well as any-gauge shotgun, .410 through 12 gauge, using #6 shot loads. Shotguns make hitting running animals a little easier.

Large Game

A variety of calibers are readily available that are suitable for hunting North American deer. It is a personal choice, but anything from .223 (with appropriate ammo) through 7mm magnum will work.

Caribou and elk require more powerful rounds than white tail deer, but .30-06 and above should be sufficient.

In Conclusion

People living normal lives, working normal jobs, going to normal places, need a self-defense weapon that fits their hands, their needs, and their budget. It needs to fire an effective self defense round, which would be anything from a .380 ACP to a .45 ACP. Any quality self-defense round in that range should be sufficient for daily carry.

The "best" handgun to carry is the one with which you are comfortable, confident, and proficient. It needs to be of such a size that it will actually be carried, not left at home or in your vehicle.

If you decide having firearms is right for you, regardless of the firearm you choose to have or carry, get some quality training, practice, and become safe and proficient with it. It may save your life.

Chapter 13

Financial Prepping

We would be remiss if we did not mention the importance of financial prepping for emergencies.

The best financial preparedness is to be debt-free, but quite honestly, most adults are far from that target. Look for the "holes in your pocket" where money seems to fall through. We have nothing against people who use thousand-dollar cell phones or buy designer clothes, if they can easily afford those things; the problems come when folks who cannot afford those things push themselves into deep debt just because they want the newest gear or flashiest fashions. Why not figure out the difference between your "needs" and your "wants"?

What are some ways we can work toward better financial prepping?

Limit debt as much as possible, and live within your means. In other words, spend less than you make. If you don't live on less than you make, find a way to cut expenses, or find a way to supplement your main income with a part-time job.

Quit using credit cards, unless you can, and WILL, pay the full balance each month. If you're carrying multiple credit card debt, pay down all the smallest balances first to get them out of your way. Transfer your largest debt to a lower-interest card if possible, or consult a no-fee debt repayment program for assistance.

Make a plan, or budget, and stick to it. Spend every dollar, on paper, before you get it. Track all your spending for a month to see where your money goes. Most of us will be surprised at how much money we spend on needless things. We've used the envelope method, each one labled, to help us construct our budgets.

Start an emergency fund. We recommend setting aside $1,000.00, used only for true emergencies, to keep from incurring more debt. Unexpected car repairs, major appliance breakdowns, or emergency travel can pop up anytime.

After having an emergency fund in place, work on paying off debt first, then slowly add to the emergency fund. Eventually, to be fully prepared, aim for having three to six months of expenses saved up. This gives you some breathing room in the event of a job loss or lay-off.

Do not spend money on unnecessary prepping equipment some sites say are "must-have" prepper items. Focus on food, water, and essentials at first. Add to your preps a little at a time, and always staying within budget.

Chapter 14

Reference Section

What follows is a reference section of various uses for common household items and other items you may wish to have, "just in case." Some are useful in everyday life around the house, and some may be invaluable in a survival event. Many of these items can be purchased for less than ten dollars, with many available at the local dollar store.

Uses For super glue

Super glue has a multitude of uses and is available in medical grade as well as standard grade.

Understand that there is some difference in medical grade super glue and the super glue purchased at the dollar store. The difference lies primarily in the purity of the medical super glue that is marketed under the names Dermabond and Nu Skin.

Dermabond is used in the hospital to close small wounds of less than 3/4 inch in length. Nu Skin is sold over the counter and can be used similarly. Both are excellent for dealing with shallow wounds, and helps keep dirt out.

No super glue, medical included, should be used on wounds with tears, jagged edges, or rough edges. It should not be used on facial wounds, deep cuts, dirty wounds, puncture or infected wounds, nor animal bites.

Other uses:

Repair tarp, tent, shoes, and garments

Repair broken tools

Repair gear, patch containers, and stop leaks

Fletch arrows

Keep rope and cordage from fraying

Stop pulls in clothes

Uses for duct tape

It has been said that half the problems we encounter can be solved with duct tape and WD-40. If it moves and shouldn't use duct tape. If it doesn't move and should, use WD-40.

The practical prepper will have a supply of both on hand, at home, and in the vehicle. Many keep some duct tape in their EDC bag or Go bag by wrapping it around a pencil, wooden dowel, or even a water bottle. Here are some uses for duct tape at home and away.

Hold things together

Make items like drinking cups

Make poncho w/ trash bags

Repair tears

Repair shoes

Attach items

Make a hammock

Emergency foot covering

Repair leaks

Wound covering

Secure bandages

Make a splint

Protect windows from storm damage

Waterproofing containers

Remove splinters

Hem plants

Cover bug bites

Build shelter w/ trash bags

Fix cracked water bottle

Fix broken poles

Line inside of shoes to keep feet warm

Trail marker

Make sling

Cover blisters

Make spear

Fletching arrows

Make cordage

Restrain people

Strap items to car or bike

Uses for bandanas

A bandana is nothing but a simple square of cloth, often brightly colored, usually cotton (the best), which can be carried in the pocket or pack, and has a multitude of uses. Some bandanas are printed with patterns, some with maps, and some even have survival tips or uses printed on them. If you don't carry at least one, you could be missing out. Here's a list of uses that come to mind. You may think of more.

Napkin

Sling

Bandage

Pre-filter water strainer

Soak and keep neck cool

Protection from the sun, keeping the sun off head and neck

Cover the face

Tie things together

Strap for other items

Flag

Scarf or neckerchief

Handkerchief

Headband / sweatband

Washcloth / towel

Secure splint

Tourniquet

Wiping rag

Toilet paper

Tinder / fire starting - with oil based insect repellant

Soak in oil to make a torch

Make a bag for small items like nuts and berries

Make char cloth

Cordage - tear into strips

Coffee filter

Noise reduction in bags and back packs

Breathing mask

Tie things together

Pot holder

To write on

Hang a flashlight in a tent

Knife sheath

Uses for trash bags

Use as a poncho – cut a hole for the head and arms

Make a rain hat – simply wrap your head as you would with a bandana

Use as an emergency shelter – duct tape several together

Keep your feet and shoes dry

Use for waterproof storage of food, clothing, and supplies

Use for ground cover under sleeping bag or blankets

As thermal underwear – yes, wrap legs and torso under clothing to stay insulated

Make a pillow by filling bag with stray or leaves

Make an emergency floatation device – fill with air and use it under your chest to float

Keep your sleeping bag dry by sliding the sleeping bag into the garbage bag

Use it to carry water – it cant support the weight of too much water, but it can easily carry a couple of gallons

Uses for bleach and calcium hypochlorite

Note: Treating water with chlorine bleach kills bacteria and viruses, but does nothing to remove chemicals, oils, poisons, or particulates.

Cholera, typhoid, and dysentery are the greatest risk after a major disaster or event where the commercial water system is disrupted.

Water must be purified before drinking. Surfaces must be kept disinfected. Food prep tools such as cutting boards, knives, and utensils must be kept disinfected as well.

Chlorine bleach or calcium hypochlorite may be used for cleaning as well as for treating water.

When using bleach, 1/4 teaspoon is added to one gallon of water. Shake and let it stand for 20 minutes. If the water is very cloudy, add a little extra bleach and let it stand a little longer.

The water will have a slight smell and taste of bleach, but the water will be safe to drink.

Calcium Hypochlorite can be used to treat water. It is available as a powder, and must be kept in a cool dry location.

Make a working solution by dissolving 1/2 teaspoon of powder in one gallon of clean water. This working solution becomes approximately the strength of bleach and is then used in a similar fashion. One gallon of working solution will treat approximately one hundred gallons of water.

Other uses for bleach:

As a disinfectant spray – mix 1-2 Tbsp with one gallon cool water and put in a spray bottle to disinfect and clean surfaces

Sanitizing small items – mix three-quarter cup of bleach with one gallon of warm water and soak items for five to ten minutes

Clean fruits and vegetables – mix one Tbsp bleach with one gallon of water in a sink or tub. Immerse fruits or vegetable for 30 seconds then rinse thoroughly

Self-defense - bleach thrown into the face of an attacker causes severe eye irritation, and even chemical burns if untreated, hopefully giving you time to escape. Note: Do this ONLY in an EMERGENCY, life-threatening attack.

Uses for hydrogen peroxide

We are all aware of hydrogen peroxides use in disinfecting cuts, scrapes, and other wounds, and even its use in hair coloring, but it has so many other uses of special interest to the practical prepper, like these:

Disinfect surfaces with a 50-50 mixture of hydrogen peroxide and water; can be put in a spray bottle for ease of use.

It kills deadly mold, especially important to those with compromised immune systems and lung function problems.

It fights ear infections - pour 2-3 drops in the ear and let it fizz for 10 minutes then turn the head and let it drain out while treating the other ear.

It can kill a sinus infection when there are no other means available. Mix two Tbsp of 3% hydrogen peroxide with a cup of warm distilled (or NON-chlorinated) water, place in a nasal spray bottle and spray each nostril twice.

Germinate survival seeds with one ounce hydrogen peroxide and one pint of water and soak overnight. Change the solution in the morning using a 50-50 mixture and change twice each day until ready to plant.

As with bleach, you can use a hydrogen peroxide solution of one-quarter cup to one gallon of water as a vegetable and fruit wash to remove chemicals, bacteria, viruses, and wax before eating them.

Uses for apple cider vinegar

Apple Cider Vinegar is a prepper's "superprep."
Here are some uses:

Medicinal:

Getting rid of leg cramps-- 1-2 Tbsp mixed in water, or taken straight up

Lower blood sugar – 1-2 Tbsp mixed in a glass of water before bed may help lower blood sugar the next morning

Lower blood cholesterol – 1-2 Tbsp mixed in a glass of water may help lower LDL (bad) cholesterol, and help raise HDL (good) cholesterol

Relieve sore throat – Mix one Tbsp with one cup of water, gargle and swallow hourly

Relieve itching – Dab directly onto affected area

Relieve upset tummy – Mix 2 tsp with a cup of water and drink

Relieve achy joints – Warm a mixture of water and honey, then add 1 oz. of vinegar and drink

Relieve sunburn pain – apply a soaked cloth or paper towel over the area

Use as an antiseptic on small cuts, scrapes, and abrasions

Relieve acid reflux – 1 Tbsp in 8 oz water, drink before or after meals

Cure hiccups – drink 1 tsp for instant relief

Cure athlete's foot – 50-50 mixture water and vinegar, apply daily, let dry

Cleaning:

Small appliances and most surfaces (sanitizes as well)

Cleaning coffee pots - run through coffee maker, then rinse well with water

As a grease cutter

Remove stains

Kills germs – 50-50 mixture in a spray bottle

Disinfect wood cutting boards

Kills and prevents mold and mildew

As a dish rinse, even in the dishwasher, to kill bacteria and make dishes sparkle

Cooking:

As a vegetable wash will kill bacteria and remove pesticides

As a salad dressing, with oil

Add 2 tsp to water before boiling eggs to make them easier to peel

As a marinade for red meat

As a base for, or addition to, sauces to make them tangy

As an additive to punch up the bland taste of soup (add after cooking)

Other uses around the house:

Cleaning rust off tools - let soak over night

Weed killer – mix 1 cup dishwashing detergent with 1 gallon vinegar

Cleaning hard water deposits and shower heads – soak in full strength

Dissolves glue, gunk, and goo

Keeps fleas off dogs - add a few drops to their drinking water

Uses for baking soda

An online search will yield many used for baking soda, but here are some that may be of particular interest to preppers. Most are best used by making a paste for direct application or by mixing with water.

Antacid or relieving ulcer pain

Bath or foot soak

Body deodorant – rub on dry

Clean coffee pots, pots, pans, boots and shoes

Denture soak

Eliminate odors - sprinkle the area

Extinguish fires

Hand cleaner

Kill slugs - dry powder

Make gravies or thicken stews

Minor burns or sunburn relief

Mouthwash

Relieve sore throat – gargle

Remove acidity from coffee – sprinkle a bit on the grounds before brewing

Soothe insect bites

Soothe the sting of poison ivy

Spike physical performance

Tenderize meats – soak ten to fifteen minutes

Uses for aluminum foil / tin foil

Tin foil is probably the most versatile item in the kitchen.

Here are many uses:

Make a pan for roasting, frying, or steaming

Scrubbing pots, pans, and grills – crumple a piece like paper and scrub away

Remove rust – same method, but takes much longer

Makeshift container for boiling water

Make a lid for pots or bottles

Wrap pots and pans to keep down soot while cooking over an open flame (dishwashing detergent works well for this - put it on thick and about half way up the pot, soot easily washes off

Insulate a cup or bottle to help keep liquids hot or cool

Collect rainwater

Making cooking packets for cooking or reheating food

Baking potatoes under a fire – wrap, bury them a few inches below ground, build a fire on top, wait a few hours, enjoy

Build a solar oven inside a box

Keep matches and small items dry

Make a signaling mirror or device

Make fishing lures by wrapping around a fishhook

Make a funnel for filling small bottles, or even gas tanks if needed

Amplify light by building a reflector around a lantern or even a candle

Ground cover under a sleeping bag

Make a faraday cage – wrap several layers around a box containing the device. DO NOT allow the device to touch the tin foil

Make a tent patch with tinfoil and pine sap

Block light coming through windows

Cut strips of tin foil, hang it with fishing line from branches to keep birds away from fruit trees, or even in the garden to keep small animals away

Sharpen scissors by folding tin foil several times and make as many cuts as you can through the layers of foil for keen edge on your scissors

And of course, for making the necessary tin foil hats to keep the aliens from controlling your mind or reading your thoughts

Tin foil may be used multiple times if you take care not to tear it. It can be folded numerous times to make it easily storable in backpacks.

As a bonus, when the foil of off the roll, you can cut the roll in half or thirds, and pack it with drier lint permeated with petroleum jelly to create great tinder for starting a fire.

Uses for salt

Of course, it makes some foods taste better.

Improve the taste of coffee by sprinkling a touch on the grounds before brewing; doing so neutralizes the acidity of the coffee, giving it a better taste

Soothe sore throats by gargling with a mixture of 1-2 Tbsp salt and one cup of water

Eggs boiled in salt-water peel more easily

Preserve meat by packing it in non-iodized salt, (iodized leaves a bit of a bitter taste)

Brining meats for a moist flavor – 2-3 Tbsp per quart of water

Prevent mold on cheese by wrapping in a cloth or paper towel dampened in salt water

Relieving insect and bee stings by covering with a water/salt paste to remove the sting

Mix 1 part salt and 2 parts baking soda to make a substitute for toothpaste

Add 2 cups Epsom salt to a tub of hot water for a soothing bath

Melting snow and ice

Put out a grease fire

Cleaning cast iron and greasy pots and pans - scrub with salt and a paper towel

Kill snails and slugs in the yard or garden

Repels ants – they do not like to walk over salt

Wash pets in a salty solution to ward off fleas

Unclog drains - pour one cup each salt and baking soda down the drain and follow with a half cup of vinegar. Let sit ten minutes then flush with a half-gallon of boiling water. Flush with hot water from the tap to finish out the job.

Clean stainless steel with a paste of salt and lemon juice, rinse well and dry

As with many items in a prepper closet, salt has many more uses than can be listed here. Hundreds of uses for these items can be found online.

Uses for tarps

There are many uses for tarps, but the two most obvious for the prepper are temporary shelter and patching holes in roofs. They have many uses around the house in "normal" times. In fact, we have three covering items in the back yard right now. Here are some uses:

Make a shelter – either a lean-to or a tent-style

Use for ground cover to keep sleeping bags dry

Gathering rainwater water into a bucket – could be a combination shelter and water collector, or placed into a hole to collect rainfall

Make a hammock by attaching between trees

Make a privacy curtain for showers or open-air outhouse

Roll a tarp tightly and tie off the ends to make a strong pull strap

Cut into strips to make cordage or straps

Make a stretcher suspended between two poles

Covering holes in the roof and broken windows (including car windows)

A makeshift poncho (as well as using a trash bag)

Cover firewood to keep it dry

To make a drag for removing harvested animals from the woods back to camp

Blue or silver tarps can be used for signaling aircraft searching for you

Uses for paracord

Paracord, or parachute cord, is lightweight and very strong and termed "kermantle rope" from the German kern, meaning 'core' and mantle, meaning "sheath." The rope is a number of inner strands contained within a protective woven outer sheath. It was originally used for the suspension line on parachutes, but today is used by the general public and is a prepper must-have. Kermantle ropes have very little, (if any), stretch and are available in a number of diameters. Both paracord, at about one-quarter inch diameter, and arborist (climbing) rope, about one-half to five-eighth inch diameter are kermantle rope.

The most popular general-use paracord is 550 paracord. It is one-quarter inch in diameter, has seven inner strands, and a tensile strength of 550 pounds. Larger sizes go into the thousands of pounds in tensile strength and are used for rappelling and for climbing by professional tree cutters.

Generally, paracord is available in fifty-foot and hundred-foot length bundles, and two hundred-fifty foot rolls. Fifty- and one-hundred foot lengths easily fit into a backpack. It is not expensive, though the 'good stuff' is higher-priced, and higher quality, than the cheap stuff available in the big box stores. For general prepping purposes, the cheap stuff does a good job, but for long duration exposure to the elements, and certainly if your life will be hanging on it, get the good stuff. If you will be rappelling, definitely get the half-inch or larger for the added tensile strength, as well as ease of gripping the rope.

Here are some of the uses for 550 paracord:

Tying off tent poles and shelter coverings

Tying tarps to trees

As cordage to secure items to belts or backpacks

As cordage to tie trees and branches together in building a shelter

Make a sling or tie a splint onto an arm or leg

Build a makeshift stretcher

Make a tourniquet

Use inner strands to make emergency dental floss

Use as a throw line to others

Make a dog collar or leash

Make a bow drill

Use inner strands for fishing line or trotline

Make a fish stringer if you are successful with your fishing

Use for hanging food and other items, like lanterns, from tree limbs

Inner strands can be used to make snares

Use for dragging gear or harvested animals

Make a strong rope with multiple strands or braids

Replace shoe or bootlaces or belt

Make a clothesline for drying clothes

Hanging a kettle over a fire

Use as a makeshift strop for your knife

Use for restraints on a bad guy

Making a replacement pull-cord for a chainsaw or boat motor

Use as a mooring line

Make a rifle sling

Make a paracord watchband or bracelet

Use as a lamp wick, in a pinch

Uses For Survival Knives

Cut

Slice

Pierce

Whittle

Pry

Cauterize wounds

Dressing game

Open tin cans

Skinning

Split/baton wood

Stab

Spatula

Fire starter (with ferro rod)

Spear

Weapon for self defense

Chopping (wood, matter for shelter)

Meal prep for cooking

Screwdriver

Tool making, (spears & stakes)

Hammer

Items for barter

This book is designed to prepare people for relatively short duration situations where we can live on our supplies for up to a few weeks or even a month or two, but lets list some barter items that may be handy to have if we ever do get into a long-term, power-grid-down, SHTF situation, if for no other reason than to get you thinking about items you may not have thought about to store for your own use.

Depending on the length and severity of an emergency situation, or SHTF, people may be wishing to barter for items they do not have or are running low in supply. Therefore, it is a good practice to store some items for this purpose, but store the items you would eventually use and can rotate over time.

Precious metals may be good in a collapsed economy, but may not be as well received in other situations. They could be harder to turn them into usable items, so therefore less attractive to many people.

Here are some other ideas:

Alcohol - both rubbing and drinking versions could be welcome barter items. Let's be frank here, the drinking kind will be more popular. Keep it in a cool place, and away from the children! Smaller quantities, such as single-shot bottles and half-pint bottles may have the highest trade value for the lowest investment. Lets face it; people are going to want to trade their item(s) for the whole bottle. This is not where you store the three-figure bottle of single malt scotch.

Tobacco products will be high value, in-demand items. Smokeless tobacco may store better and stay moist longer, where cigarettes may dry out quicker. Both need to be kept in a cool location.

Water filtration – Sawyer minis and Lifestraws will be in high demand if the water system stops flowing.

Coffee/Tea-- The fact is, many of us are addicted to caffeine and it would be a sad day for those around us if we ran out and could not get it. It also provides a pick-me-up and is a good soothing comfort beverage. Keep it cool and dry. Store the good stuff, too, not the instant kind (unless that is what you normally drink).

Food/Water/MREs are not that expensive to stock and can be used, bartered, or given out in humanitarian aid.

Ammunition causes a lot of disagreement in the prepper world. Some say not to barter ammo, but we say 'know your trading partner'. (If we did trade it, we would not allow loading it until out of our sight). Mark has stocked up on .22 long-rifle ammo for years, believing it could become the currency of the day in an extended grid-down situation. It does exactly that in William Forstchen's post-apocalyptic thriller, "One Year After." The dentist charged two dollars in silver coin or ten .22 long rifle shells, and said he preferred the ammo. Most folks have at least one .22 rifle in the closet, which can be used hunting small game and, though not the best choice, for home- or self-defense. Ammo becomes rather scarce, especially after the news covers major natural disasters, or sometimes, closer to election time. During the COVID-19 crisis, ammo seemed to go away with the toilet paper. DO NOT barter firearms unless it is a much-trusted family member or close friend.

Baby supplies - babies are going to need formula, tearless shampoos, diapers and LOTS of wipes.

Batteries are needed to keep flashlights and radios running. Store extra; they have a long shelf life.

Bleach & hydrogen peroxide has so many uses that it will be valuable for barter – see Uses for these items.

Blankets

Books, board games, and decks of cards

Candles, oil lamps, and lamp oil - people have to be able to see after dark.

Cast-iron cookware – many today do not own cookware that can be used over an open fire

Chapstick, lip balm, and sunscreen – if it all goes down for a long period of time, we're going to be outside a lot.

Chocolate and snack foods

Cleaning products, detergent

Clothing of various sizes

Cloth bags or reusable shopping bags for foraging or scrounging

Condoms - yep, have to keep that baby-boom low

Duct tape

Emergency blankets

Fire starters, lighters, matches, and lighter fluid

Fishing and hunting supplies - hooks, lines, weights, inexpensive rods and reels, camouflage, deer scents, grunts, and turkey calls could prove valuable

Flashlights and Headlamps

Flavored drink mixes – helps with the taste of bleach-treated water

Food items you raise in the garden, or fresh eggs if you keep chickens, as well as canned or dried foods, and baking goods like flour, baking powder, cornstarch, cornmeal, cake mix, biscuit mix etc.

Fuel of any kind – gas, diesel, kerosene, propane, lamp oil, even charcoal and firewood

Handheld radios will keep the family or neighbors in touch while out, or use for trade

Hand tools – shovels, axes, hammers, nails, screwdrivers and pliers, etc.

Honey – it literally lasts forever, as in never spoils; bee-keeping could become profitable

Hygiene supplies, toothpaste, toothbrushes, soap, shampoo, and especially feminine products

Medical supplies, first-aid supplies, and OTC medications, such as acetaminophen and ibuprofen, Benadryl, anti-diarrhea meds, and allergy meds as well as antiseptic creams, and multi-vitamins

Rain jackets, suits, and ponchos

Skills can be bartered as well as items – gunsmith, mechanic, barber, gardener, carpentry, hunting and fishing will be in demand; almost anything except the 'art' of being a politician can be bartered. Making moonshine might again become a common 'occupation'

Sewing supplies, fabric and yarn

Soda – as addictive as coffee

Spices, Salt, Pepper, and Sugar

Tarps and sheets of plastic

Tents – small or large could be very valuable to anyone without a roof over their head

Tin foil/Aluminum foil - see the list of uses for this handy item

Toilet paper – could have made some awesome trades during the COVID-19 toilet paper crisis

Water containers, and bottled water

Water filters, coffee filters (for straining sediment out of water, and water purification tablets

Ziplock bags – keeps small items together and dry, can be used to carry water and store food

This is by no means an exhaustive list, but it may give you an idea of things you might need for your own preps, as well as for barter. Most of these are inexpensive and store well. Add a few here and there, starting with things you do not already have.

Items that will likely disappear quickly

Items that will quickly disappear from shelves after an event are somewhat event-specific; the following items disappear quickly depending on the event:

Bread, milk, and sandwich materials

Bottled water

Camping supplies, tents, stoves, fire starters

Candles, matches, and lighters

Charcoal, lighter fluid, and charcoal grills

Coffee, snack foods, and canned soups

Flashlights, and batteries

Fuel – both gasoline and propane

Generators, gasoline containers, and gasoline

Insect repellent

Lamp oil, wicks and lamps

Paper towels

Portable heaters and bottles of propane

Ready to eat food

Seasoned firewood

Tarps

Toilet paper and hygiene supplies

Vinegar, bleach, and cleaning supplies

Water filters

Prepper and SHTF Radio Frequencies

The following frequency information was compiled in 2013 from public domain sources. It is in the public domain, but reprinted here with permission.

PREPPER & SHTF COMMUNICATIONS
2 WAY RADIO FREQUENCIES

BAND	CHAN	FREQ.MHZ	NOTES
FRS	3	462.6125FM	PREPPER FRS
GMRS	20 / 675	462.675+FM	PL 141.3 REPEATR
MURS	3	151.940 FM	PREPPER MURS
CB AM	3 AM	26.985 AM	PREPPER CB
CB AM	9 AM	27.065 AM	EMERGENCY CB
CB SSB	36 USB	27.365USB	SHTF SURVIVAL
CB SSB	37 USB	27.375USB	PREPPER CB SSB
CB FREEBAND	38 GAP	27.378USB	SHTF SURVIVAL
CB FREEBAND	E 2 HI	27.425USB	SHTF SURVIVAL
LOWBAND VHF	LOW	33.400 FM	SHTF SURVIVAL
LOWBAND VHF	PKDOT	42.980 FM	PREPPER LOW
HAM VHF	2 M	146.520 FM	HAM CALL SIMP
HAM VHF	2 M	146.550 FM	HAM PREPR SIMP
HAM VHF	6 M	51.000 FM	HAM PREPR SIMP
HAM HF	10 M	28.305USB	HAM PREPR TECH
HAM HF	20 M	14.242USB	HAM TAPRN
HAM HF	40 M	7.242LSB	HAM TAPRN NET
HAM HF	60 M	5.357USB	HAM SHTF NVIS
HAM HF	80 M	3.818LSB	HAM TAPRN NET
LAND SAR VHF	SARFM	155.160 FM	SEARCH&RESCUE
MARINE VHF	16	156.800 FM	SAFETY CALLING
MARINE VHF	72	156.625 FM	MARINE PREPPER
AIRCRAFT VHF	GUARD	121.500 AM	EMERG DISTRESS

Chapter 15

Glossary Of Prepper Terms, Abbreviations, and Acronyms

These terms are included for a better understanding for those who wish to read prepper forums, listen to podcasts, and as a reference for everyone.

72-Hour Bag - Supplies and tools that would enable you to survive an emergency situation for three days

BIB - Bug In Bag

BOB - Bug Out Bag, when you absolutely have to leave

BOL - Bug Out Location

BOV - Bug Out Vehicle

BUG IN - Staying put, hunkering down, and sheltering in place

BUG OUT - Take what you can and leave

CME - Coronal Mass Ejection

EMP - Electromagnetic Pulse

EDC - Every Day Carry

FIFO - "First in, first out" used in reference to food stores and supplies

FUBAR - Screwed up beyond all recognition

GDE - Grid Down Event

GET HOME BAG - 72 hr bag, to get you home if you're stranded

GO BAG - the bag that goes with you, preferably daily

GO KIT - deployment bag for going to help others

GOLDEN HOARD - Swarms of desperate people who want what you have

GOOD - Get Out Of Dodge

INCH Kit - "I'm Never Coming Home" Kit

IFAK - Individual First-Aid Kit

MAG - Mutual Aid Group

MRE - Meals Ready To Eat

OPSEC - Operational Security

OTG - Off The Grid

POLLYANNA - Denies there is a problem or trusts that "the government" will supply their needs. Used in reference to thought and actions.

PSK - Personal Survival Kit

PREPS - Food, tools, and supplies stored in preparation of an event

RTE - Ready To Eat

SHEEPLE - People who blindly follow the masses in thought and action

SHTF - "Stuff" Hits The Fan (Keeping it clean)

SOL - S**t outta luck

SOP - Standard Operating Procedure

TEOTWAKI - The End Of The World As We Know It

WROL - Without Rule Of Law

YOYO – You're On Your Own

ZOMBIES - Slang term for the unprepared that may try to aggressively take your resources. These people will do harm to you and your family to get what they want.

Other References

There are quite many good prepping podcasts ranging across many topics. Some specialize in specific areas of prepping others are more general. An internet search will provide many more hosted both on their own servers as well as commercial podcast sites such as Stitcher and Spotify. Here are a few podcasts we listen to from time to time:

www.casualpreppers.com

www.prepperwebsitepodcast.com (Todd Sepulveda)

www.blogtalkradio.com/survivalmedicine (Nurse Amy and Dr. Bones

www.thesurvivalpodcast.com (Jack Spirko)

www.armchairsurvivalist.com

www.intherabithole.com   (Archived)

www.todayssurvival.com   (Archived)

Websites and forums we frequent from time to time:

www.prepperwebsite.com

www.apartmentprepper.com

www.backdoorsurvival.com

www.doomandbloom.com

www.expertprepper.com

www.theorganicprepper.com

www.urbansurvivalsite.com

www.surviopedia.com

www.thesurvivalistblog.net

www.modernsurvivalonline.com

Notes:

Thank you for reading this book.
Please take a moment to leave a review. These really help increase the availability of the book.

Check out our website at: www.practicalprepping.info

Or find us on Facebook at: "The Practical Prepper"

Email us at mark@marklawley.us

www.ingramcontent.com/pod-product-compliance
Lightning Source LLC
Chambersburg PA
CBHW060539160726
47991CB00001B/399